The Mob File

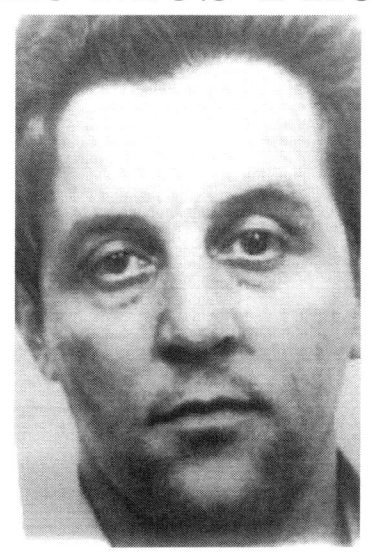

The Illustrated Guide to the Mob in Vegas.

The Mob Files
The Illustrated Guide to the Mob in Vegas.

By
By John William Tuohy

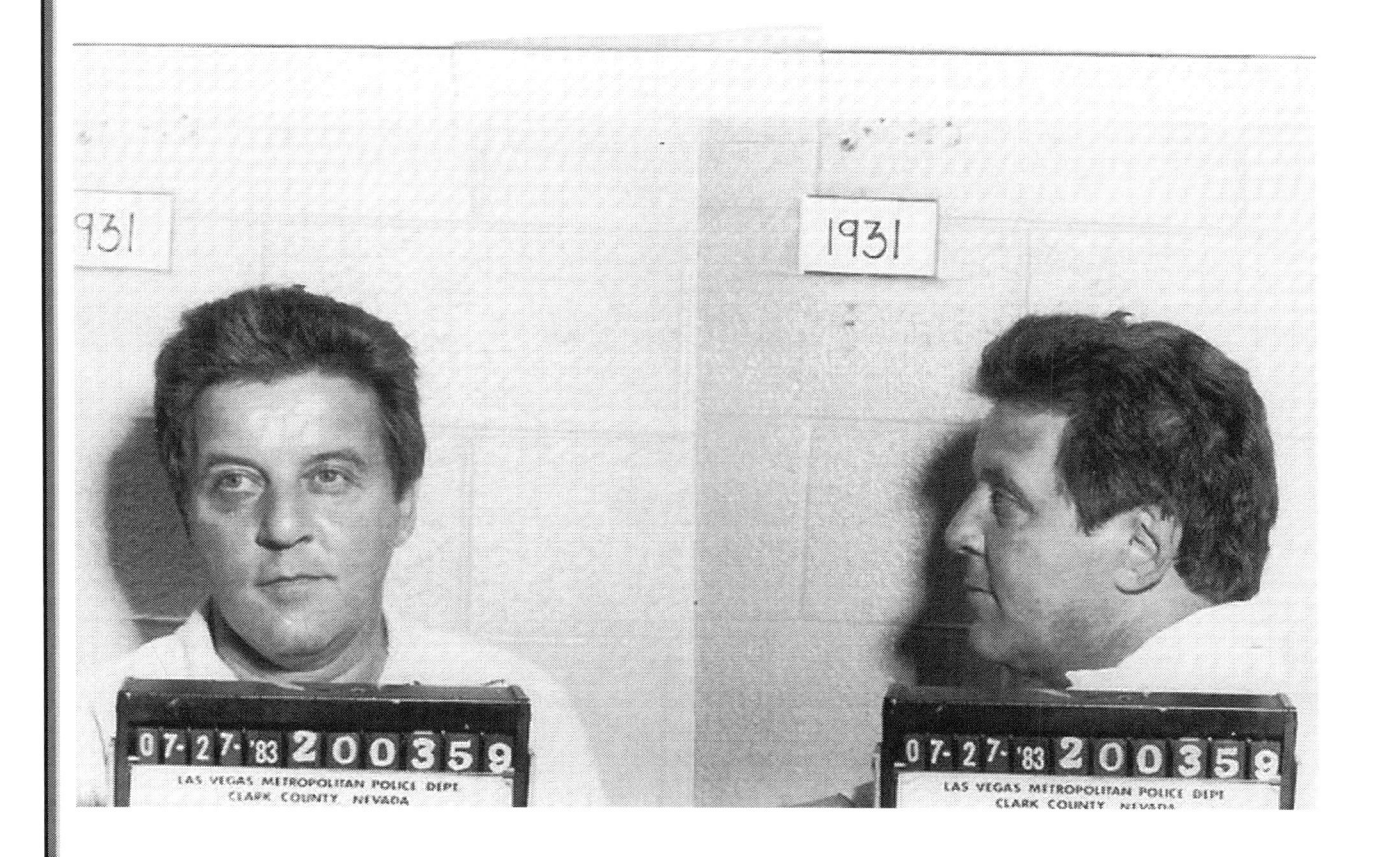

Balistrieri Frank P: AKA Frankie Bal. Born May 27, 1918 Died February 7, 1993. A hood based in Milwaukee who was deeply involved in the Vegas casino skimming operations in the 1970s through the 1990s. College educated (He attended law school but didn't graduate) he married into the mob by wedding the daughter of Milwaukee boss, John Alioto. He took control of the family in about 1961.

On March 20, 1974, Balistrieri met with Kansas City mobsters Nicholas Civella and Carl DeLuna in Vegas to discuss having the Mobs Vegas front man Allen Glick sell half his corporation's ownership to Balestrieri's sons John and Joseph Balistrieri for $25,000. Balistrieri believed that since he had found Glick in the first place (Glick was a college friend of one of Balestrieri's sons) and had helped Glick secure the financing to purchase his Vegas casinos from the Teamsters pension funds (some $62.75 million in all) that the Balestrieri's were entitled to the points in Glick's corporation. But the Civella's disagreed over each other's share from the skimming operations and Chicago's Joey Aiuppa and his Underboss Jackie Cerone were brought into mediate the dispute for a quarter of the take. Almost ten years later, in 1983, Balistrieri and his two sons were indicted with bosses from Chicago, Cleveland and Kansas City for skimming over $2 million from the Stardust and Fremont Hotel and Casinos. On May 30, 1983, Balistrieri was sentenced to thirteen years in prison and fined $30,000 (his sons were both convicted of extortion from a vending machine businessman the previous month). Two years later, he was also convicted of skimming an estimated $2 million of the gross income of the Argent Corporation from syndicate casino operations and distributing the money between the Kansas City, Chicago, Milwaukee and Cleveland mobs. The judge sentenced the hood to an additional 30 years in federal prison. Balistrieri was granted parole in 1992 due to poor health. He died a year later of natural causes (heart attack) at age 74.

*****

Baron Charles: AKA Babe Baron was an interesting figure in the underworld. Baron, a former prize fighter, owned a successful car dealership and eventually would hold the rank of brigadier-general in the Illinois National Guard. Baron was arrested twice for murder including the killing of bootlegger James Walsh in 1929 and Gus Winkler in 1932. During the Kefauver hearings, Baron was identified as an associate of John Roselli and as a former general manager of the Havana Riviera in pre-revolutionary Cuba. He was granted a gaming license in 1960 and served as the official greeter of the Sands casino under Joseph "Doc" Stacher. He was also a close associate of Patrick Hoy, a Henry Crown employee of General Dynamics who was later able to arrange a job for Sidney Korshak at the Hilton Hotels. A former general manager of the Havana Riviera in pre-revolutionary Cuba, he was one of the first to be granted a gaming license by the Gaming Control Act in 1960 and served as the official greeter of the Sands casino under Joseph "Doc" Stacher.

*****

Barzotinni, Dante: AKA Tino Barzie. Frank Sinatra Jr.'s manager. He purchased $50,000 worth of boasted airline tickets from gangster Henry Hill to fly Sinatra Jr. and a group of eight friends around the country. Barzotinni was caught, arrested and convicted.

*****

Becker Edwin: Born 1922 California died in Las Vegas in 2007. Becker claimed to be a licensed private investigator from Los Angeles, although he primarily did publicity work for several San Francisco nightclubs and wrote a celebrity column for two California newspapers. In 1955 Becker became a public relations director for the Riviera Hotel and Casino in Las Vegas, and claimed to have worked closely with Gus Greenbaum, the manager of the Riviera and the Flamingo. In 1959, Becker floated into a partnership with "two men who were running a con deal involving Laundromats and stolen credit cards." as the FBI reported. According to Becker, one of the men was an associate of Los Angeles mob boss Joe Sica. Becker also withheld his criminal past from the FBI. He had twice been the subject of criminal investigations, the first resulting in his conviction on misdemeanor charges for having stolen "around $200" from a nightclub photographer with whom he was acquainted. He served 60 days in jail for the theft. He was the subject of an SEC desist order in conjunction with the 1959 investigation.

During the early 1960's, Edwin Becker did investigative work in Los Angeles for Julian Blodgett, a former FBI agent and former chief investigator for the District Attorney of Los Angeles County. However, on November 5, 1962, Blodgett advised the LA FBI office that Becker was unreliable and had been lying to him and then terminated his services. Becker claimed that while working for a victim of a mob swindle that involved Billie Sol Estes that he travelled to Louisiana and was introduced to Carlos Marcello, the crime boss of New Orleans.

Becker made the remarkable and highly dubious claim that on a second meeting with the extremely secretive Marcello on September 11, 1962, in a farmhouse at Churchill Farms, the 3,000 acre plantation owned by the crime, that the crime boss told him that he "clearly stated that he was going to arrange to have President Kennedy murdered in some way [and] that his own lieutenants could not be in on the actual hit."

According to Becker, the low key, slow to anger and very mundane Marcello cried out "Take the stone out of my shoe! Don't worry about that little Bobby son of a bitch!" he shouted, "He is going to be taken care of." Later in the conversation, Becker said, Marcello said that to rid himself of Robert F. Kennedy he would first have to remove the President. Any killer of the Attorney General would be hunted down by his brother; the death of the President would seal the fate of his Attorney General. When Becker was interviewed by the FBI on November 26, 1962, he made no mention of the Marcello threats, which according to him, had been uttered by the gangsters just thirty days before the interview. The statements were elevated to FBI Director Hoover directly and an investigation was launched from the top down to verify Becker's remarkable claims. The FBI determined that Becker was an unreliable source. The bureau also concluded that Carlo Roppolo, the hood whom Becker claimed had introduced him to Marcello "was regarded as rather shiftless...a problem person who had little credibility with Marcello"

According to the FBI, Sidney Korshak, the mobs west coast lawyer and a major power within the Chicago Outfit, had been discussing Becker and "Korshak inquired as to who Ed Becker was and advised that Becker was trying to shake down some Korshak's friends for money by claiming he is the collaborator with Reid and that for money he could keep the names of these people out of the book" The memorandum also stated that Sidney Korshak had further stated that "Becker was a no-good shakedown artist," An FBI report from November 27, 1962, in stated that Becker made up "stories" and invented rumors to derive "possible gain" from such false information and that a man who had been acquainted with Becker had referred to him as a "small-time con man."

*****

Berman, David: Las Vegas Casino Boss. AKA Davie the Jew: Born 1903. Died 1957. Berman was born in Odessa, the Ukraine, the son of a former rabbinical student. Berman would remain steadfastly religious throughout his life, even helping Bugsy Siegel to fiancé the first synagogue in Las Vegas. (A four-bedroom house) When Berman was still a child, the family moved to South Dakota, as part of a Jewish resettlement program funded by Baron Maurice de Hirsch. From there the Berman's moved to Iowa. By 1916, Berman was running his own gang in Sioux City and eventually moved to Minneapolis where he developed a working relationship with the New York based Genovese Crime family. Berman prospered with prohibition and gambling. Working with him, in those days and throughout his entire criminal career was his brother Chickie and Israel Alderman AKA Ice Pick Willie. Berman enlisted in the Canadian army in World War 2 (He was rejected by the US Army based on his felony record) and served in an elite reconnaissance ranger's outfit.

After the war, Minneapolis elected a young racket busting Hubert Humprey as mayor. Humprey effectively pushed Berman, now a wealthy man, out of the city and into the waiting arms of Meyer Lansky and Bugsy Siegel in Las Vegas. Reportedly, the Genovese family in New York, which had investment money with Siegel, insisted that Berman and his men, be included in Siegel's dealings in Vegas. Before leaving Minnesota, Berman married a former dancer named Gladys Ewald, a German –American who converted to Judaism. She took her own life, at age 39, shortly after her husband's death, by an overdose of sleeping pills. Her daughter Susan believed that she was murdered for refusing to give up her late husband's shares in casinos.

Meyer Lansky

It was Berman and his manager, Gus Greenbaum who walked into the Flamingo Hotel on June 21, 1947, only hours after Bugsy Siegel was shot dead and announced "We're taking over" (Contrary to film legend, Berman did not shout the news. Rather he spoke the words softly). By the early 1950s, Berman, his brother and Ice Pick Willie Alderman were either owners or, or partner's in the Rivera and was involved with the Flamingo, the El Cortez and the El Dorado casinos. Berman died in 1957 after entering the hospital for a simple surgery. Susan Berman also believed her father's death was also under mysterious circumstances. Susan later wrote a book, Easy Street, about her father and growing up as what she termed "A Jewish Mafia princess in Las Vegas" Susan Berman was a troubled woman whom friends described as "smart, intense, and complex woman who challenged the boundaries of friendships and relationships. She was also the victim of many phobias, including crossing bridges, riding in elevators, and staying above the third floor in hotels; and at one point, she rashly attempted to kill herself." A gifted writer who was in and out of mental asylums throughout most of her adults life, she was murdered in her home Las Angeles on December 24, 2000.

*****

Biase Anthony Joseph: Born September 6, 1909 Died September 21, 1991. Baise worked in both the Omaha and Denver mobs between the 1930s and 1950s. Arrested on numerous charges including bookmaking, burglary and armed robbery in the Rocky Mountain area during the 1930s, he eventually became involved in illegal gambling operations in San Francisco, Los Angeles and later in syndicate casinos in Las Vegas. Biase later became an associate of Vito Genovese as the New York crime boss extended his criminal operations in the western United States and, following the conviction of mobster Anthony Marcella on charges of narcotics and tax evasion, succeeded Marcella as head of the Denver based crime syndicate.

*****

Blitzstein Herbert: Las Vegas Gangster. AKA Fat Herbie. Born November 2, 1934. Died January 6, 1997. On July 13, 1967, a bookie named Arthur "Boodie" Cowan (Born 1921) was shot dead for withholding a street tax to Tony Spilotro. Cowan, of 7307 Crawford Avenue in Lincolnwood, was found in the trunk of a car a week after he was reporting missing. The cause of death wasn't clear because the body had been so badly mutilated. Spilotro choose Blitzstein, (Who then lived at 7334 North Ridge Avenue in Chicago) to take his pace and so began a thirty-year association that ended in both Spilotro and Blitzstein's death.

Fat Herbie

   After a series of arrests for bookmaking, Blitzstein moved out to Las Vegas sometime in the early 1970s and went to work for Spilotro's brother John, who would eventually open the Gold Rush, a jewelry store that was also center for fencing stolen goods.

   Over the years, after Tony Spilotro moved out to Vegas, he was seldom seen without the massive Blitzstein by his side. At this point, Blitzstein was making his living primarily as a burglar as were most of Spilotro's so-called Las Vegas based Hole in the Wall Gang. The 300 plus pound gangster also suffered from heart problems and diabetes that caused him to have two heart bypass operations and eventually to have several toes on his right foot removed. Things went from bad to worse when he was forced to plead guilty to four federal indictments that included charges for credit card fraud and income tax evasion.

   Released from prison in 1991, he returned to Vegas…Spilotro was long since dead…and almost immediately faced a hearing to have his name entered into the Vegas Black Book (Which is actually green) which restricted him from entering the casinos as "A person of unsavory reputation"

Undaunted, Blitzstein opened a loan sharking business and ran a series of simple auto insurance schemes which turned a healthy profit. No longer protected by Spilotro or the Chicago Outfit, young Wise guys from the LA and Buffalo families started to extort money from Blitzstein.

On January 6, 1997, the gangsters simply grew tired of taking payments from Blitzstein and decided to take over all of his operation. Mafia contract killer entered Blitzstein's home and fired three bullets into him, killing him.

*****

Bioff Willie His name is barely known today, but for almost a decade he was at the forefront of what remains the largest extortion case in the history of American criminal justice, that set the foundation of modern organized crime.

When the national depression knocked the bottom out of Chicago's once enormous prostitution racket, Bioff, a pimp, started to shake down Fulton Street shopkeepers, restricting himself to the Jewish stores and thus allowing George Brown, another goon whom Bioff knew only in passing, to work the Gentile side of the street.

Since Brown and Bioff collected their payoffs from Fulton Street at the same time of the day, on the same day of the week, they starting talking and soon formed a partnership dubbed B&B, for Brown and Bioff.

Together, Brown and Bioff merged their shake down operations on Fulton Street and expanded their control of the stagehand's union by increasing dues by $5.00, and then pocketing the increase for themselves. Since that plan worked out so easily, over dinner one night they came up with another plan to raise more money, by threatening the theaters with a strike. Bioff came up with an even better idea. Instead of collecting money once from the theater owners, they would sell them a "a no strike guarantee," which they would collect monthly.

The two hoods approached Barney Balaban, owner of Chicago's largest and most successful movie house chain, Balaban and Katz theaters. Sam Katz, who would go on to own MGM Studios, and Barney Balaban, who would one day run Paramount, had begun operating nickelodeons as teenagers, and in 1916, were among the very first to produce silent films. Balaban was a tough, two fisted, self-made man and when Bioff and Brown showed up with their extortion threats, he personally threw them out of the building, no small chore.

Bioff and Brown talked about it and decided that they entered into the shakedown the wrong way because they were unsure of themselves and nervous, and it showed. A few days later, they went back, more self-assured, and promised Balaban that if they didn't get their way, there would be a strike, it would last for months . . . unless Balaban gave $20,000 to B&B Enterprises.

To soften the blow, Bioff told Balaban that the money was to go directly to unemployed union members, for emergency help, like a soup kitchen. It was a lie of course. They intended, in fact they did, steal every penny of the money. But Bioff was smart enough to know that if Balaban gave the $20,000 to a charitable cause, like a soup kitchen, then the company could write the money off of their corporate tax bill and win public admiration at the same time.

Barney Balaban was also a shrewd dealer. He quickly figured out that neither Bioff nor Brown would keep any written documents of the transaction since they intended to steal the money anyway. That meant that Balaban and Katz could fork over $20,000 to Bioff and Brown's "soup kitchen" and tell the government they had donated $100,000 and then pocket the additional $80,000 for themselves. The beauty of it was, Bioff and Brown would swear that they had been given any amount Balaban said they had been given. They had to. They had no other choice.

Brown and Bioff got the twenty grand. In cash. It was delivered by Balaban's lawyer Leo Spitz, who, before handing the money over, reached into the suitcase and pulled out $1,000 and stuffed it in his pocket "for carrying charges," he explained.

Like the small timers they were, after the payoff, Bioff and Brown went out on the town and gambled away thousands of dollars in a mob-run casino inside the Loop, a place called the Club 100, run by Nick Circella, a surly hood who worked directly for syndicate boss Frankie Rio, a former Capone bodyguard.

Rio and Circella were in the club that night, both of them had known Bioff for twenty years. As they sipped their espressos from the owner's table, and watched Bioff lose another grand on the roulette wheel, Circella wondered aloud, "where two losers like Willie and Brown would get that kind of cash." Rio was thinking the same thing and ordered Circella to find out what the two had been up to. Two days later, Frankie Rio called Bioff and Brown, and told them they were going to see Frank Nitti's home. After the federal government railroaded Al Capone off to prison and out of power forever, his place was taken by Frank "The Enforcer" Nitti, who got the position more out of attrition due to thinning mob ranks than anything else.

Bioff and Brown, dressed in their best suits, waited in the drawing room of Nitti's twenty-room mansion, having arrived 15 minutes early. George Brown was terrified. He was certain the summons to Nitti's place was the kiss of death, although he didn't know what he done to deserve it. But Bioff, always the smarter of the two, saw the summons for what it was, the opportunity. Otherwise, he reasoned, if they had crossed Nitti in some way they didn't realize, they would have been dead already, left in a back alley in the loop someplace, not waiting in a living room on a Saturday morning.

After a half hour, a young, smartly dressed thug they didn't recognize came out and led them into a large, formal living room where Phil D'Andrea, former Capone bodyguard, Paul Ricca, Charles "Cherry Nose" Gioe, a top executive in the outfit and Louis "Little New York" Campagna were waiting. The boss himself, Frank Nitti, sat in his desk chair, glaring up at Brown and Bioff. "Where'd you get the money?" Nitti snapped. "And don't you fuck'n lie to me."

George Brown was too terrified to speak, so Bioff did all the talking, explaining the entire shakedown in a matter of minutes, but blaming everything on his partner, George Brown.

Nitti understood everything, even before Bioff had finished talking. He also saw the big picture at once. There were hundreds of movie theaters in pre-television Chicago, thousands in Illinois and tens of thousands across the United States. The potential was endless.

Nitti leaned back in his oversized leather chair and declared that he was cutting the outfit in on B&B's deal for 50%, although he would later increase that to 75% and then 90%. From that amount, 10% of the gross went into the mob's general treasury and the rest was divided up among those who had invested in the scheme. Furthermore, Nitti said, he was taking the stagehand's union from Bioff and Brown and reducing them to his bagmen within the union. They, Brown and Bioff, would handle the day-to-day problems in the local, but if they had any serious troubles, they were to report them to Nick Circella. When he was finished talking, Nitti leaned up towards his desk and said, "All right, now get out."

The Chicago outfit had always had its eye on Hollywood. It started with Capone. Just before he went to jail forever, Big Al had called a general meeting of the boys and told them he intended to extend his power westward to Los Angeles and ordered Nitti to draw up a plan to look into taking over Chicago's enormous entertainment industry. Then the Taxmen came around and slammed away Capone for good, but Nitti never forgot the plan to invade Hollywood.

Now, in 1933, Nitti looked at Hollywood and its stars and producers with skeletons in their closets, and said, "The goose was in the oven waiting to be cooked."

He was right, too. Los Angeles was a wide-open city. Disputes were settled in gunshots, wildcat gangsters simply moved into town and bribed politicians, elections were rigged by competing gangs. The district attorney, Baron Fritts, was already on his way to becoming one of the country's most corrupt lawmen and the police chief, Jim Davis, was a loudmouth clown who carried two six-gun revolvers, and, was so corrupt that a detective's badge could be purchased for five dollars. The Mayor, Frank Shaw, admitted to newspapers that he rigged elections and placed his brother in charge of a spy squad within the police department that kept track of, and intimidated, his enemies. Compared to Los Angeles, Frank Nitti's Chicago was a bastion of order. But that was Los Angeles. Hollywood was a different place, hell it was a different planet.

An avid reader of the daily financials, Nitti learned that the movie business was ripe for extortion, for a wage increase shakedown, because the depression had hit the industry hard, and profits were off. The danger in low profits for the studios, was that the entire motion picture business was only 15 years old. Other, older and more established businesses might be able to withstand a drain on its cash, but the Hollywood studios weren't ready for the same trial. Still, even with sagging profits and a shaky foundation, movie pictures were one of America's top ten grossing industries. Every day, tens of millions of dollars poured into its bank accounts, and Nitti and the syndicate wanted a piece of the cash. With control of the national union entertainment unions, they would get it, just the way Capone had planned it back in 1929.

A few days after the meeting with Brown and Bioff, Frank Nitti met with his council at the Capri restaurant inside Chicago's loop so he could introduce his plan to take over the entire union on a national level.

Over lunch, Nitti pulled out the newspaper clipping he had on Balaban's nationwide operation and said he had spent the morning on the phone with Lucky Luciano in New York. He told the boys, Paul Ricca, Louis Campagna, Frankie Rio and Nick Circella, that he and Luciano had decided that their mobs, New York and Chicago, would work together to take over the movie business across America.

The entertainment business was too big, Nitti explained, and covered too many miles, for Chicago to try and take it alone. Besides, he added, Luciano and the other New York families already controlled the East Coast Stage Workers and projectionists' locals whose control was vital to a successful takeover.

Nitti said that he and Lucky had decided that the first place to start was with Barney Balaban. They would send Bioff back into Balaban's office with a demand for a 20% increase for the projectionists. Nitti said that he expected Balaban to refuse to pay. When he did, the New York syndicate, working the Chicago syndicate, would arrange a general strike against all of Balaban's theaters on the East Coast and the Midwest.

Nitti said that the projectionists would be out of work for a few weeks and the theater chain would close down. Then, at the last minute, Nitti would send in George Brown to act as peacemaker and stabilizer who would end the strike through peaceful negotiations, while at the same time getting the projectionists a small raise. With that done, the mob would run him for the Stagehand Union presidency in the next election.

That's what they did and it worked. The strike ended and George Brown was the hero of the working man and the studios alike.

In June of 1934, the union held its national election in Louisville, Kentucky. With the weight of the entire national syndicate behind him, George Brown was elected national President of the IATSE, the union that, effectively, controlled the entertainment business, and Willie Bioff was appointed Brown's "Special Representative", at a salary of $22,000. The Chicago mob's takeover of a giant American industry had begun.

After the convention, Frank Nitti called Bioff and Brown into his office and told them that he had decided that it was best if they, Bioff and Brown, moved out to California where they would be closer to the studio's offices and production centers. The pair did as they were ordered, and while Brown spent most his time locked behind his office doors drinking beer, Willie Bioff made himself busy. In less than three months, he took $250,000 in cash from the movie moguls at Warner, 20th Century Fox, Paramount, everybody paid, all of it in cash, wrapped in brown paper bundles.

When Bioff arrived in Hollywood, Chicago representative Johnny Roselli met him at the train station and gave the little pimp an orientation tour of the city and the industry he was about to bring to its knees.

Johnny Roselli 1925

As they drove through Beverly Hills, Roselli stopped in front of Joan Crawford's mansion and told Bioff an interesting story. Roselli said that right after he had landed a job for himself as a staff investigator for the Hay's office, he was given a case to look into by MGM Studios. It seemed that when one of their rising stars, a real beauty named Joan Crawford, was a starving 19-year-old actress, she had appeared in several pornographic films.

Now in 1935, some freelance extortionists said that they had a print of the film and were shaking down MGM for $100,000 to hand over the film negative.

The bosses over at MGM considered the investment they already had in Crawford, added that with her box office appeal and potential, and decided that it would be less expensive to pay the extortionists off, but not for $100,000.

The bosses handed the case over to Roselli and told him to contact the hoods and offer them $25,000 in cash to back off. The studio would write the money off of their taxes as a business expense.

Roselli contacted the hoods, a group of small timers, and explained that he represented not only MGM Studios but the Mafia as well. He told them that if they ever contacted the studios or Crawford again, he'd kill them.

Case solved. Roselli pocketed the studio's $25,000, produced the film negative and the threats stopped.

A few years later, Roselli and Bioff met again. After a complicated series of federal wage laws and disputes with the movie studios over a 20% increase in salaries, the independent entertainment unions decided to strike on April 30, 1937. A strike by these unions could close down film production across California. If that happened, the syndicate would never collect on their control over the unions.

The studios wanted the strike broken and they wanted the syndicate to break it. Frank Nitti argued against any involvement, but this time things were reversed, the studios pressured the outfit, and took their case to Lucky Luciano and Longy Zwillman in New York. Luciano and Zwillman talked to Nitti and, reluctantly, Nitti agreed to break the strike.

Nitti handed the job to Johnny Roselli who hired a squad of twenty leg-breakers from Chicago and San Francisco and marched them to the Hollywood police station where they were given gun permits and then brought them to the studio gates where the striking union membership was gathered.

Armed with baseball bats and steel chains, Roselli's goons threw themselves at the striking union members who took a severe beating that first day but were back on the strike line the next morning.

The outfit goons continued to dole out beatings for several more weeks before the union brass imported its own sluggers, some hired from local gyms, others brought in from the Long Shoreman's union in New York.

Herb Sorrell, a labor organizer for the union recalled that "there were numerous fights, and it was a rough strike. In the six weeks that it lasted, there were several killed and I didn't know how many injured. In fact it was the roughest strike I ever participated in." Realizing that brute force wouldn't win the strike, Roselli told George Brown and Willie Bioff to call a press conference with the studio bosses and declare the striking union's leadership as "communist infiltrated."

Then all-powerful Screen Actors Guild voted to ignore the union's picket lines and eventually the smaller unions either disbanded or became a part of the larger organizations. The Federation of Motion Picture Crafts was destroyed, the outfit's union reigned supreme.

Nitti, who always expected the worst in everything, was amazed to find out that he didn't need a ramrod to knock down Hollywood's golden gates. He just knocked gently and they sprung open for him. The reason for that was that Hollywood, as Nitti would quickly learn, was, like him, all about money.

Although it later became known as the Bioff and Brown extortion scandal, it wasn't really extortion, at least not in the classic sense, because the studio heads, by paying off Bioff and Nitti's not to raise prices, were actually saving money, perhaps millions of dollars over what they would have to have paid a legitimate union in wage increases. Furthermore, the scandal benefited the studios in other ways because the mob, for everything that was evil about it, usually kept its word once it was paid, and the mob had agreed not to raise labor prices. That promise assured the studios that productions would finish without stoppage or a problem from IATSE's 12,000 members, and as result of a toothless union, the studios fired workers at will and pushed others to work over time without compensation; as a result, films were made for less money because not as many people were needed. In fact, the payoffs to the mob, saved the studios about $15,000,000.00 in what they would have paid out in wage increases.

With the mob behind them as a working partner, the studios no longer had to deal with Communists who had infiltrated the locals and stirred up trouble, or the small time thugs who kept coming back for more nickels and dimes or the weak labor leaders who couldn't keep their promises because they had no real control over their membership. Producers knew that with the mob in charge, they could get a picture wrapped up on schedule because there would be no strikes and as an added bonus the mob ordered Bioff & Brown to raise prices for live theater, opera, plays and concerts, which were competing with the movie business. Everybody, except the membership, was happy.

Joe Schenck was one of the founding Fathers of Hollywood.

Joe Schenck got involved with, in fact he almost helped to design, the mob's shakedown of the Hollywood studios in April of 1936. Unlike the gangsters who lived from day to day on their incomes, the studio heads relied on budgets.

Bioff's surprise visits were starting to tax the bottom line. The studio heads gathered together and decided to let Nick Schenck come up with a plan that would satisfy the outfit and the studios.

Schenck was about to pay Bioff anywhere near a million dollars, however, he did a quick take on Bioff and decided that he could be bribed. Schenck told Bioff that the DuPont representative in California wanted to increase his raw film business with MGM and the other studios. He said that DuPont was willing to pay Bioff a 7% commission to act as the designated "agent" between DuPont Chemical and the Hollywood studios; better yet, all of the actual footwork would be done by a "sub agent" assigned by DuPont, all Bioff had to do was cash the checks.

Bioff agreed to the deal under the conditions that his income never fell under $50,000 a year and that Schenck was not to mention the commission deal to anyone else, meaning Frank Nitti, or his west coast boy, Johnny Roselli.

Schenck called the other studio heads, explained the situation and all of them agreed, reluctantly, to switch their business from Eastman Kodak raw film to DuPont. In the last part of 1937, the raw film commission deal that Schenck had put together gave Bioff $159,025 in commissions, an enormous amount of money for that time.

Flush with more cash than he ever dreamed possible, Willie Bioff "went Hollywood." He started to wear expensive clothes and carried three diamond-studded, solid gold, union business cards in his wallet. Using mostly union funds, and by applying yet another special collection on the studios, Bioff was able to raise enough funds to buy a massive ranch. Here, he grew alfalfa and flowers and relaxed in his mahogany-paneled mansion where, although he could barely read, Bioff had a pine-knot library filled with the world's greatest books and rare and expensive volumes. He bought a Louis XV bedroom and rare Chinese vases and fancied himself a connoisseur of rare vases and had a kidney shaped swimming pool built in the back yard for his seven children.

Willie Bioff's new ranch and the unusual methods he used to finance it weren't missed by Montgomery Clift, the Screen Actors Guild President, who had his own informants within the studios. Clift figured, correctly, that the ranch was a payoff from Schenck to ensure Bioff's secrecy. Then, one of Clift's informants provided him with a copy of the check that Schenck had made out to Willie Bioff for $100,000. Clift reported the deal to the IRS and eventually Schenck was secretly indicted for tax evasion.

When questioned about the check he had written to Bioff, Schenck said it was a loan. Later on, he made the mistake of testifying to that under oath. When the government was able to prove that Schenck paid Bioff the money as a means to avoid taxes, he was indicted on several counts of tax evasion. Schenck, always the businessman, decided to cooperate with the government in exchange for his a light sentence.

The government agreed and Joe Schenck sat before the grand jury and outlined the entire scam. The grand jury eventually found Schenck guilty of tax evasion and he was sentenced to five years at a federal prison, but Joe Schenck wasn't just anybody. He wasn't going to serve out his term in jail and the whole world knew it. He served just under a year, was granted a Presidential by Harry S. Truman and then went to running his studios as though nothing had happened.

Based on Schenck's testimony, the federal grand jury issued subpoenas for all the major studio heads, but still, up until almost the very end, the government had no real clear understanding of the extent of Bioff's extortion scam or the fact that the mob, New York and Chicago, were involved. Then Harry Warner stood before the grand jury and filled in the gaps. Warner's evidence was enough to put everybody involved behind bars.

On May 23, 1941, Brown, Bioff, Paul Ricca, Frank Nitti, Nick Circella, Charlie Gioe, and Phil D'Andrea were indicted for extortion and tax evasion. Willie Bioff had no intention of doing any jail time. He called US Attorney Boris Kostelanetz from a jailhouse visitor's phone and opened the conversation by saying, "This is Bioff . . . Okay, Boris, what do you want to know?"

Bioff laid out the entire scheme for Kostelanetz, times, dates, places, names and amounts; of course he worked a good deal for himself first. In exchange for his testimony, the government agreed to let Bioff keep the money he had stolen over the past decade, furthermore, he would walk away from any charges against him.
After three weeks, Bioff finished giving his testimony to the grand jury, and when he was finished talking, indictments were handed down for Johnny Roselli, Frank Nitti, Paul Ricca, Louis Campagna, Charlie Gioe, Phil D'Andrea, Ralph Pierce and Frankie Diamond.

There was a trial, but none of the outfit members took the stand in their own defense, the case against them was that overwhelming. On December 30, 1943, the verdict against them was returned. They were each found guilty and sentenced an average of ten years in federal prison plus $10,000 fine and were liable for the back taxes owed. It was, as the Chicago Herald American wrote, "The total demolition of the Chicago syndicate."

Frank Nitti never went to trial on the Bioff charges, because a day before he was indicted, he took a .45 and blew his brains out, just as he had always promised he would if he ever faced another long prison sentence.

Paul Ricca decided he wasn't going to do any jail time either. Working through Campagna's wife they were put in touch with a Missouri legislator named Edward "Putty Nose" Brady who in turn placed them in contact with a St. Louis lawyer named Paul Dillon who wasn't new to the mob. He knew Murray Humphreys, the Chicago outfit's collector, very well and had defended two IATSE union officers at Humphreys' request, after they were caught beating up a movie theater owner in St. Louis in 1939.

Dillon, then 68, also had strong political connections to the Missouri underworld including Johnny Lazia, the Kansas City gambling king who was killed in 1934 and Tom Pendergast, the boss of Kansas City.

But, what Ricca needed Dillon for was his close, personnel relationship with President Harry Truman. In 1934, at the personnel request of Missouri crime king, Boss Pendergast, Dillon had acted as Harry Truman campaign manager in his race for the senate. Dillon had also worked as a lawyer for Boss Pendergast, and represented Pendergasts's chief lieutenant, "Smiling Johnny" Lazia, on an income tax fraud charge.

Dillon loved the power, the money and the clout working with these clients gave him. He bragged, often and loudly, that he could visit Truman at the White House whenever he wanted to.

In October of 1945, Dillon met "Putty Nose" Brady, who had ties to the Chicago outfit that went back to the Capone organization. With Brady at the meeting was an ex-prizefighter, and occasional Brady business partner, James Testa. Dillon, according to Testa, provided them with a price list with a set amount of money he would need to have each of the Chicago hoods released by using his influence in Washington with the Truman White House.

While Dillon was collecting his bribe money from Testa and Brady, another lawyer named Maury Hughes of Dallas, traveled to Washington and met with Attorney General Clark. The two men had grown up together. Shortly after the meeting, the Attorney General requested the gangsters transfer to Leavenworth.

For decades no one in law enforcement was clear on what hand Clark had played in the transfer or where Hughes fit in until Murray Humphreys summed it all up when he, knowingly or unknowingly, told an FBI microphone on October 16, 1964. "Attorney General Tom Clarke was, he always was, 100% for doing favors . . . the guy Maury Hughes who went to Clarke was an ex law partner (from Dallas) and then the scandal broke."

Humphreys also said that another lawyer they hired, Bradley Eben, was paid the astounding fee of $15,000, an enormous amount of money in 1945, to "consult" on the case. Eben's mother was a Truman White House employee who worked as a liaison between Attorney General Clarke and the President.

On August 6, 1947, Dillon, made an application for parole for Ricca, Gioe, Campagna and D'Andrea. The application was strongly opposed by Boris Kostelanetz, the special assistant attorney general, even the federal judge who passed sentence wrote to the attorney general Clark objecting to the application for parole. But, on August 13, 1947, exactly one week after the application for parole had been placed, Ricca, Campagna, Gioe and D'Andrea were released on parole. A three man, federal parole team voted unanimously to release the hoods and acted so quickly and quietly on their decision, that the parole office in Chicago didn't have time to submit its standard analysis of the case, which meant that the parole team reached its decision having seen only a fraction of the inmates' records.

The public, especially in Hollywood and Chicago, were outraged over the hoods' release, and Representative Fred E. Busbey confronted the Parole Board members and asked them, directly and without mincing words, if it was true that they had accepted a $500,000 bribe to grant paroles to the hoods. Remarkably, not one of the parole board members denied accepting the money, nor would they admit to it.

The House Expenditures Committee recommended that the four hoods be sent back to prison and that their paroles be revoked. The carefully worded report held that the paroles had been given under highly questionable circumstances, and identified Dillon and Hughes as being personal friends of President Truman and Attorney General Clark. It concluded, however, that it could find no grounds to indict the President, Clarke or Hughes and could find no evidence that anyone had been bribed but concluded that "A good Samaritan" had spent big money to get the hoods released.

That "good Samaritan" turned out to be Tony Accardo, who ordered each of his capos to visit the attorney's office and drop a specific amount on the desk to free Ricca and the others. They were to say nothing except, "This is for Paul Ricca," drop the money on the desk, and leave. By the end of the day, Ricca's lawyers had the $200,000 needed to pay off his tax lien. Now the hoods' Attorney could truly say that "a bunch of strangers and good and concerned citizens donated the money."

When Louis Campagna was called before committee he said he didn't know who any of the estimated forty-two men were who dropped the money on the lawyer's desk or what their motivation was.

"Do you believe in Santa Claus?" Representative Hoffman asked Campagna.

"Yes, Yes. After all this," Campagna said "I suppose I do . . . I mean if you were me, wouldn't you?"

In its final report, the Congressional Committee charged to look into the entire mess wrote: "The syndicate has given the most striking demonstration of political clout in the history of the republic."

Willie Bioff moved to Arizona, where he lived under the name Willie Nelson, Nelson being his wife's maiden name. Contrary to what's usually written, Willie Bioff wasn't hiding out in Arizona. In fact, he worked at the Riviera Casino in Vegas as the entertainment director for Gus Greenbaum, Chicago's man in Nevada.

Outgoing, likable and very rich, Willie was a natural for politics, and was soon popular within the golden elite of Phoenix society, which is how he met Barry Goldwater, in November of 1952.   The two men became fast friends.

Goldwater, a brigadier general in the Air Force Reserve, flew Bioff and his wife all over the state to attend various parties, and Willie landed a steady flow of cash into Goldwater's political campaign chest. Bioff even loaned Bobby Goldwater $10,000 for a farming investment in Southern California.   A month before the Mafia killed him, Willie Bioff and his wife, Barry Goldwater and his family, vacationed together in Las Vegas.

In 1955, Peter Licavoli and Paul Ricca, boss of the Chicago mob, started to shake Bioff down for cash. Willie paid off for a while, but then remarked that he might go to the federal government for help.   The next morning, Bioff stepped into his Ford pickup, stepped on the gas and was killed instantly by a bomb planted under the hood of the truck. Both of his legs and his right arm was blown off.

*****

Anthony Brancato, (Above) killed Aug. 6, 1951, 1648 N. Ogden Drive, Hollywood, along with Anthony Trombino in the "Two Tonys Murder." Jimmy "The Weasel" Fratianno eventually confessed to the killings.

Black Book: Nevada's Black Book (not actually black but silver) is an attempt to keep organized crime out of casinos. Officials add the names of known crime figures to the book, and then any book member commits a crime simply by setting foot in a casino. The casino also commits a crime if it fails to report gambling in its facility by a Black Book member. The book is only 36 pages long but lists some of the most notorious names in gambling crime since its creation in 1960. It was born out of the fear that if Nevada couldn't keep organized crime out of gambling then Congress would eliminate the industry completely through high taxes. Eleven names were drawn up in the original list, consisting of individuals defined as having a "notorious and unsavory reputation which would adversely affect public confidence and trust that the gaming industry is free from criminal or corruptive elements."

Under state gaming law, anyone can be placed in the Black Book if he/she has a felony conviction, committed a crime involving moral turpitude or violated gaming laws in another state; failed to disclose an interest in a gaming establishment; willfully evaded paying taxes or fees; or has a "notorious or unsavory" reputation established through state or federal government investigations. Originally, the process of placing someone on the list was an administrative function without due process, but nominees are now allowed to attend a public hearing to dispute their inclusion. Once listed in the Black Book, if members are caught entering a restricted gaming establishment they face a gross misdemeanor charge. Exemptions include airports, bars and stores with 15 slot machines or less and no gaming tables. As well, casino operators who refuse to report gambling activity by a Black Book member can face fines and licensing problems. The legality of the Black Book has been challenged numerous times and survived both state and federal courts.

Original 11 persons included in the Nevada Black Book of excluded persons. (Persons excluded from entering casinos in the State of Nevada. The Black book is actually silver)

1. John Louis Battaglia. Removed 1975.
2. Marshall Caifano (Since died)
3. Carl Civella. Removed 1996.
4. Nicholas Civella. Removed 1983.

5. Michael Coppola. Removed 1975.//
6. Louis Dragna.
7. Robert L. Garcia. Removed 1986.
8. Sam Giancana. Removed 1975.
9. Motel Grzebienacy. Removed 1975.
10. Murray Llewellyn Humphreys. Removed 1975.
11. Joseph Sica.

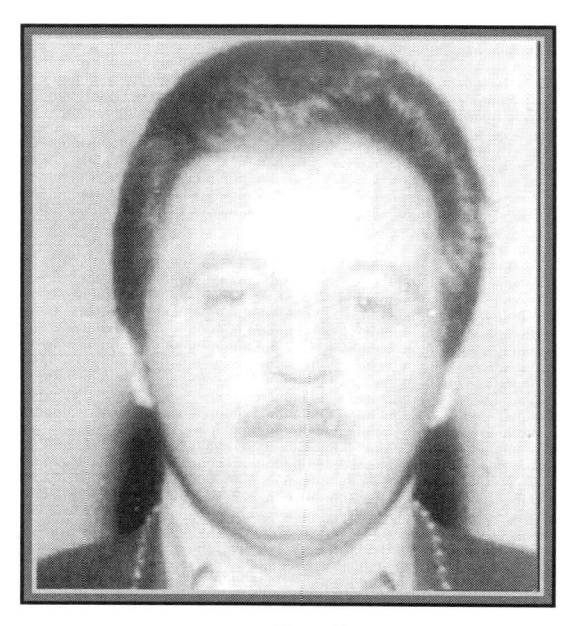

*****

Bolles, Don: US Senator McCain's father in law was James W. Hensley, an Arizona businessman who fell in with the wrong crowd a while back, and ended up taking the rap for a wheeler-dealer named Kemper Marley, Sr. over a liquor violation case back in 1948. Although Hensley was represented by the best defense Arizona cash could buy, the services of future Chief Justice of the United States Supreme Court, Justice William Rehnquist, he got slammed away for a whole year. When Hensley strolled out of the joint, Marley bought his silence with a lucrative Phoenix-based Budweiser beer distributorship. On a sweltering summer day in 1976 when Don Bolles, a reporter for the Arizona Republican Newspaper, stepped into his Datsun, put his foot on the peddle and was blown to bits. Parts of the reporter's body were found ten feet from the burning car.

Don Bolles car after the bombing

Bolles had been poking into Arizona's local and state governments and discovered a land fraud ring, influence peddling, and shady deals that appeared to lead to the very top of Arizona's power structure and to Senator Barry Goldwater's doorstep.

If the purpose of murdering Bolles was to cover a series of crimes, it was a big mistake. An enraged news media descended on Arizona, determined to uncover the facts behind the Bolles killing.

The investigation led to a Phoenix liquor magnate and one time Bookie named Kemper Marley Sr., who had ties to Arizona's resident Mafia Prince, Peter Licavoli.

Marley was a major financial and political power in the state and wanted to take back his seat on the Arizona Racing Commission. He had already been appointed to the post in 1976 by the Governor, only to resign several days later when his ties to organized crime surfaced. The reporter who made the connections between the mob and Marley was Don Bolles. Although never charged with the murder, most reporters on the scene believed that Kemper Marley ordered Bolles' murder. Their suspicions were confirmed when John Adamson, an alleged burglar and arsonist, confessed to blowing up Bolles.

During the trial, a witness named Howard Woodall testified that Adamson told him Bolles was killed because he'd uncovered evidence of a loan swindle involving Marley, Barry and Robert Goldwater and Harry Rosenzweig.

The Bolles-Marley connection to the Goldwater brothers was only one of the many associations made over the years between the Senator and the underworld.

Robert Goldwater, the Senator's brother, was a longtime friend of Moe Dalitz, the man who truly built Las Vegas.

Dalitz was present at the Atlantic City crime conference in 1929, and at the all-important 1943 power summit at the Waldorf Astoria.

Dalitz was an early investor in Arizona real estate, with some of his first deals going back to 1933.

In 1943, it was Dalitz who introduced mob Underboss Peter Licavoli, Sr. to the state.

Licavoli loved the place and purchased a massive Tucson ranch and he and Bobby Goldwater eventually went into the restaurant business, with Licavoli putting up the financing. Another pal with a questionable background, who was close to the Goldwater camp, was Willie Bioff, labor extortionist, paid goon, pimp and government informant.

In 1943, Bioff testified against the top leadership of the Chicago mob about their role in a massive Hollywood extortion scandal. That testimony resulted in convictions for mob boss Paul Ricca, Johnny Roselli and others.

In exchange for selling out his partners, Bioff walked away from prosecution a free man and got to keep the millions he had stolen as well.

Willie moved to Arizona, where he lived under the name Willie Nelson, Nelson being his wife's maiden name.

Contrary to what's usually written, Willie Bioff wasn't hiding out in Arizona. In fact, he worked at the Riviera Casino in Vegas as the entertainment director for Gus Greenbaum, Chicago's man in Nevada.

Outgoing, likable and very rich, Willie was a natural for politics, and was soon popular within the golden elite of Phoenix society, which is how he met Barry Goldwater, in November of 1952.

The two men became fast friends.

Goldwater, a brigadier general in the Air Force Reserve, flew Bioff and his wife all over the state to attend various parties, and Willie landed a steady flow of cash into Goldwater's political campaign chest.

Willie even loaned Bobby Goldwater $10,000 for a farming investment in Southern California.

They were close.

A month before the Mafia killed him, Willie Bioff and his wife, Barry Goldwater and his family, vacationed together in Las Vegas.

In 1955, Peter Licavoli, Moe Dalitz's old pal, and Paul Ricca, boss of the Chicago mob, started to shake Bioff down for cash.

Willie paid off for a while, but then he started making noise about going to the feds through his new pal, Barry Goldwater.

The next morning, Bioff stepped into his Ford pickup, stepped on the gas, and was blown to kingdom come.

Barry Goldwater showed up for the funeral and denied, with a straight face, knowing who Willie Bioff really was.

Later, when the pressure continued, the Senator justified his relationship with the onetime pimp by saying it was an attempt "to gather information about labor racketeering for a government study."

After that, came the Newman scandal.

Mike Newman, was a childhood friend of the Goldwater's and operated a huge gambling racket, completely unhindered by the law, in Phoenix.

Police suspected that Newman's money man was Gus Greenbaum, but the connection was never made.

The building he operated out of was owned by Harry Rosenzweig, who was a close friend of both Gus Greenbaum and Willie Bioff. Rosenzweig was also the state Republican chairman, Phoenix Man of the Year, and Barry Goldwater's financial and political mentor.

When Newman's gambling operation was eventually closed down and charges were brought against him, Barry Goldwater used his considerable political power to get Newman a lenient sentence and outstanding prison conditions. Goldwater's troublesome brother, Bobby, was said to be Newman's best customer.

*****

Bompensiero Frank: Frank "the Bomp" Bompensiero was born in Milwaukee in 1905 and eventually made his way west to California. In 1937, Benjamin "Bugsy" Siegel, representing the national syndicate let it be known that West Coast gamblers would have to split their profits down the middle with him. One gambler who held out was Lew Brunemann, who had aspirations of controlling all the gambling in southern California. In July 1937, Bompensiero and one of his men found Brunemann strolling along Redondo Beach. The mobsters walked up behind him and put three slugs in his back, Brunemann lived. A while later, on October 25, Brunemann was having his dinners at the Roost Café, in Redondo Beach restaurant, with one of his nurses. Bompensiero and his gunman Leo "Lips" Moceri, a former member of Detroit's Purple Gang. Moceri said later "I've got a forty-five automatic and the place's packed with people. I walk right up to his table and start pumping lead. Believe me, that sonovabitch's going to be dead for sure this time. "Bomp's supposed to be by the door, watching my back to make sure nobody jumps me. I turn around and I see this football player ... coming at me. Bomp's nowhere in sight. Now I'm either going to clip this (guy) or he's going to knock me on my ass. So I blast him and run out, and there's Bomp already in the fucking car ... waiting for me. That guy showed me his color. If you ever work with Bomp, get him out in front of you instead of behind you." The police arrested the wrong man for the Brunemann murder.

On February 28, 1938, Moceri and Bompensiero kidnapped Phil Galuzo off a Los Angeles street. Bompensiero gave Galuzo a vicious beating and then shot him six times. After that Bompensiero left the west coast and hid out in Tampa under the protection by the Trafficante Family. When he returned to Los Angeles in June 1941, the murder charges against him were dropped due to lack of evidence. After Bugsy Siegel's murder in June of 1947, Los Angeles Mafia boss Jack Dragna attempted to take over the local gambling operations. Almost everyone fell into place except Mickey Cohen, one of Siegel's top men who was heavily into narcotics.

On Aug. 18, 1948, Jimmy Fratianno and his family visited Cohen's haberdashery shop to pick up tickets to the musical "Annie Get Your Gun." Outside a Mafia hit squad was waiting. Inside, Fratianno shook Cohen's hand and left. As soon as Fratianno was gone, Cohen, who had a clean fetish, retreated to a bathroom to wash his hands. Once outside, Fratianno signaled Frank DeSimone and Bompensiero and three other men pulled up. Bompensiero, carry a shotgun, shot Cohen's bodyguard Hooky Rothman in the face. Two other Cohen associates inside the store, Al Snyder and Jimmy Rist, were slightly wounded. Cohen escaped. Moceri later said "It was Bomp's contract, and he blew it. Listen, (the others) didn't know Mickey from a lamppost, but Bomp did. They go in there and blast away at Al Snyder thinking he's Mickey. Then they shoot him in the arm, for Christ's sake. While this going on, Mickey's in the shitcan, standing on top of the sink. They didn't pump one slug through that door. Like a bunch of cowboys, they panicked and ran out instead of finishing the job." In the very early 1950s, Jack Dragna appointed Bompensiero boss of the San Diego territory. Bompensiero kept office at nightclub they owned together, the Gold Rail.

In the early 1950s, Fratianno met with Bompensiero to discuss plans to murder Frank Borgia, an ex-bootlegger still tied to Dragna. Gaspare Matranga was trying to extort money from Borgia who lodged a complaint with Dragna. Of course Dragna was in on the shakedown; otherwise it never would have happened in the first place. When Borgia wouldn't pay, Dragna ordered Bompensiero to murder Borgia. Anthony Mirabile brought Borgia to Joe Adamo's house. Once inside Mirabile grabbed Borgia while Bompensiero and Fratianno pulled a rope around Borgia's throat and pulled from opposite ends, choking him to death. In 1955, Bompensiero was convicted on three counts of bribery and was sentenced to three-to-14 years in San Quentin. He served five.

Fratianno was transferred San Quentin as well and Bompensiero made the mistake of telling him that he killed "Red" Sagunda, an ex-Cleveland thug who was operating in San Diego. In the meantime, Jack Dragna died in 1957 and was succeeded by lawyer-turned-mobster Frank DeSimone who drove the LA family into the ground. When he died in 1968, the group was taken over by Nick Licata, would prove to be even a weaker boss then DeSimone.

Bompensiero despised Johnny Roselli, the west coast representative of the Chicago mob in Los Angeles and Las Vegas, "These two guys (from Detroit) were having a feud and they went to see Joe Zerilli, each wanting the other guy clipped. So Mike Polizzi came to see me and this was strictly between us, nothing to do with the L. A. family. They tell me who they want clipped but I've got to do the job alone. As it happens I know the guy. So one night I see him at a party and I pull him aside. I says, 'Look here, you've been having this problem and the old man's given me the contract. I'm going to clip this guy but I'm going to need your help.' Now this guy's all happy, see, and I tell him I've got a bad back and I need him to dig the hole. We go out to this fucking place I've picked out ahead of time and this guy starts digging the fucking hole. Works like a sonovabitch, this guy, sweating bullets. So finally he says, 'How's that? Deep enough.' I'm sitting down, resting, so I get up and I says, 'It's perfect.' He starts climbing out of the hole and I shoot the cocksucker in the back of the fucking head. Back down he goes in the hole and I fill it in." According to Bompensiero, he was supposed to receive a percentage of the profits from the Frontier Casino in Las Vegas as compensation for the hit. When Detroit reneged, Bompensiero went to see Johnny Roselli to make things right. Roselli ended up with a percentage of the casinos gift shop. Bompensiero never forgot the slight or forgave Roselli.

In 1967, Bompensiero became an informant for the FBI. In December of 1967 Johnny Roselli was charged with fleecing members of the Beverly Hills Friars Club out of $400,000 in rigged gin-rummy games. Seach, a member of the gang, who was granted immunity as a government witness if he testified against Roselli. Roselli learned about the deal and asked Fratianno to find Seach and kill him. He never did because Bompensiero notified the FBI and Seach was moved out to Hawaii.

In the early 1970s, Bompensiero did business with Anthony "Tony the Ant" Spilotro, the Chicago mob's new overseer in Las Vegas but otherwise continued to be a malcontent in the LA operation. When Nick Licata died in 1974, Dominic Brooklier took over the Los Angeles Mob and a year later, put out a contract on Bompensiero but Mob gunmen couldn't track him down. When Brooklier went to prison, Louis Tom Dragna, the nephew of Jack and the acting family boss announced that he was making Bompensiero Consigliere of the Los Angeles Mafia. It was little more than a trick to drag Bompensiero out into the open. They would wait to kill him.

Dominic Brooklier (Above both photos) and Tom Dragna (Bottom)

The FBI learned that Fratianno was getting into the pornography business so the agency set up a dummy company called Forex and had Bompensiero tell Fratianno about the company. Several days later, Fratianno learned that Forex was an FBI sting operation. Fratianno called Bompensiero and demanded to know where he had learned about Forex and why he wanted the outfit to get involved. Bompensiero lied and said that the information from a local pornography storeowner. When Fratianno told Bompensiero to bring the store owner to him, Bompensiero said that the owner had been killed several days before. They knew he was lying. On February 10, 1977, the 71-year old Bompensiero he was shot and killed by Thomas Ricciardi. Jimmy Fratianno eventually became an FBI informant and would later be forced into the Witness Protection Program. Suffering from Alzheimer's disease, died in his sleep at the age of 79 in June of 1993.

*****

Buccieri Frank AKA The Horse, AKA Frank Russo, AKA Big Frank Born January 23, 1919. Died March 8, 2004. The brother of Chicago mobster Fifi Buccieri, he was a boss in Cicero in the late 1`950s and early 1960s He had one criminal conviction, a petty theft charge dating back to 1936. When called before a Federal grand jury, Brother Fifi Buccieri responded to questions about his Brother Frank's relationship with a former Playboy centerfold and about the expensive horse which Frank had given her, by saying "I take the Fifth on the horse and the broad." Buccieri was sent to the West Coast on the general agreement of the major Mafia families, to watch over their substantial investments there while the Los Angeles mob collapsed. Otherwise he operated quietly out of Palm Springs.

*****

Irwin Weiner was a professional front man for the Chicago mob and answered to his childhood friend Milwaukee Phil Alderisio. Weiner's chief function was to act as a g-between for the Outfit and the Teamsters in arranging a series of fraudulent loans made out to Weiner's paper corporations. Weiner was a childhood friend of Jack Ruby, the Chicago born gunman who killed Lee Harvey Oswald. Ruby and Weiner spoke by phone a few weeks before John F. Kennedy was killed in Dallas.

*****

Buccieri, Eddie: A distant cousin to Chicago hoodlum Fifi Buccieri. A dispute with Las Vegas front man Allen Glick caused enforcer Tony Spilotro to shoot Buccieri dead in a Vegas parking lot.

Fifi Buccieri, a major power in the Chicago Outfit under Sam Giancana

*****

Cellini Dino: (Born Dino Vicente Cellini) Born 1918. Cellini was Meyer Lansky's top Lieutenant in Cuba and ran Lansky's in Tropicana casinos in the late 1950s. Years later, he ran casinos in the Bahamas and another in England with film star George Raft. Underworld legend has it, although completely lacking any sources that Lansky sent Cellini, the son of an immigrant barber and an alleged Made member of the Mafia, to a mob conclave to plead with the bosses not to assassinate President John F. Kennedy. Another story, probably a more accurate story, has Cellini bribing former members of Batista's intelligence services, not to murder Kennedy. Cellini's brother Eddie, 'an international gambler' was reported to be involved in dealings with Nathan Landow, a Democratic fundraiser for Al Gore's 2000 Presidential bid. Landow was also involved with a scandal involving Bill Clinton while Clinton was in the White House.

*****

Citro, Francis Jr: Citro was an acquaintance of both Anthony Spilotro and Joey Hansen. In December of 1990, Citro was "invited" to appear before the Nevada States Gaming Commission to explain why he should not be included in the Black Book of persons excluded from the states casinos. Citro showed up for the hearing in a tuxedo, with his pregnant wife and their children in tow. When asked about the tuxedo, Citro explained that he had never been formally invited to join anything before and wanted to show his respects. The commission barred him from the gaming business anyway.

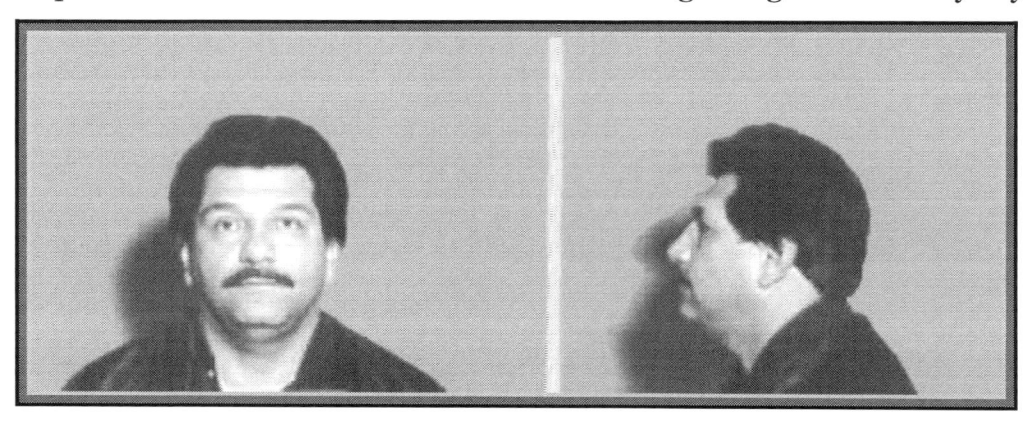

*****

Cohn, Harry: Studio owner. AKA King Cohn, a nickname he had given himself. Cohn rose out of the slums of New York, to become the head of a major American film studio. But, the streets never left him and Cohn was as rude, crude and vulgar. He regaled in his own ignorance and his ability to offend.

As a producer, many people in the business considered Cohn to be the meanest, most vindictive and hard-nosed man in Hollywood, with a sadistic power fixation. After visiting Italy in 1933 and befriending Mussolini, (he would keep a signed photo of the Dictator on his desk until the war started) Cohn returned to Hollywood and had his office remodeled after Il Duce's.

His massive desk was raised on a dais from which he could look down at the writers and directors who worked under him; men like the talented Ben Hecht who despised Cohn and his famous temper tantrums, and gave him his nickname "White Fang."

Starlets who worked for Cohn had to endure at least one "hell week" of sleeping with Cohn if they intended to make it at Columbia, and, in 1948, it was Marilyn Monroe's turn. Cohn had always said that he considered Monroe "a second string no talent with tits" and that the only reason he hired her was that Tony Accardo, then boss of the Chicago mob, owned Monroe's career and had told Johnny Roselli to force Cohn into signing Monroe on with Columbia Studios.

Cohn had his way with Monroe of course, giving her bit parts in exchange for the favors, but one day when she was summoned to his office for sex, the fickle and moody actress simply refused to go. She told Cohn that she was madly in love with Frank Sinatra, a man Cohn never liked anyway.

Word about Monroe's defiance got around the studios, and Cohn fired her. As for Sinatra, who was at the bottom of his career and probably had no idea what the erratic Monroe had told Cohn, he was blacklisted off the lot.

At about this same time, Cohn was producing the film "From Here to Eternity" and Sinatra, who had read the novel, desperately wanted to play the part of a character named Maggio, a slightly built but tough Italian-American. He was perfect for the part, and, if he got it, it would put him on top again . . . and Sinatra badly needed to get back on top again. He was out of work, owed $109,000 in back taxes, his voice was gone, and his fans had left after he divorced his long-suffering wife and married the actress Ava Gardner.

Sinatra, again without any knowledge of the rift that Monroe had caused between him and Cohn, met with Cohn on Columbia's lot and asked for the part of Maggio but Cohn refused. "Cohn looked at me," Sinatra said, "funny like, and said 'Look Frank, that's an actor's part, a stage actor's part. You're nothing but a hoofer.'" Nobody really knows what happened next.

According to Sinatra, who was already dogged in his career by the Dorsey story, Cohn changed his mind about giving Sinatra the part, after Frank agreed to take the role for $1,000 a week, a substantial drop from his usual price of $150,000 a film, even though nobody in Hollywood was willing to pay him a fraction of that price. The other version of what happened was depicted in the film "The Godfather" when a decapitated $600,000 horse head ends up in the bed of a Hollywood producer named Jack Woltz. Woltz, according to the story line, refused to hire singer Johnny Fontiane, a Mafia don's godson, for a film "that will put me back on top again" and it does too, just as the role of Maggio landed Sinatra back on top.

What is certain is that after Cohn turned Sinatra down for the part, that Sinatra called Frank Entratta, who fronted at the Sands Casino for the powerful New York Mafia Don, Frank Costello and his partners, labor goon Joe Adonis and Chicago's Paul Ricca and Tony Accardo.

Entratta was a close, personnel friend of Harry Cohn, they were regular fishing partners on weekends, but even the phone calls from Entratta didn't budge Cohn to hand the part to Sinatra.

Then, according to Johnny Roselli, Entratta went directly to Frank Costello on Sinatra's behalf, and, working with Chicago's permission, Costello contacted Johnny Roselli out in Las Vegas and asked him to look into "this Cohn problem."

Johnny Roselli knew Cohn, they had first met back in the early 1930s right after both arrived in Hollywood and Roselli was still running numbers, and selling the occasional shipment of heroin around the studio lots. Cohn took an immediate liking to Roselli, which was easy to do, Roselli was chosen for the job by the bosses because he was likable.

Soon Roselli was a regular visitor to Cohn's house. On almost any weekend, the gangster could be found lounging around the pool or playing tennis on most weekends in the late 1930s and when Cohn separated from his first wife in 1936, Roselli found him a penthouse to live in at Sunset Plaza, a luxury bungalow complex at the opposite side of Columbia Studios, and Roselli rented the ground floor from Cohn. Once, when Roselli remarked that he wanted to get out of the rackets and go into show business, Cohn offered him a position at Columbia as a producer at $500 a week, about four times the average national income.

However, Roselli turned it down, saying "I get more than that from the waitresses who take bets from me." The two men were so close that the FBI, who were tailing Roselli off and on over the years, figured he was Cohn's bodyguard.

The core of the friendship was gambling. Cohn was a gambler and Roselli was his bookie, in fact Cohn was so obsessed with horseracing, he even had Roselli arrange to have a transmitter for the horse racing results brought directly into his office at the studio. He and Roselli shared a betting pool of over $15,000, an enormous amount of money in the Thirties, and Roselli, under orders from Chicago, made sure that Cohn got all the right information on which races were winners and which were losers.

Roselli also helped Cohn on the business front, like the time in 1932 when Cohn decided that he wanted to take control of Columbia Studios from his brother, Jack, who controlled the company finances from the corporate office in New York.

The problem was that each brother owned a third of the company with the difference being held by a businessman named Joe Brandt, one of Jack Cohn's early partners. The Cohn brothers would meet occasionally in New York, but relations between them were strained, and toward the end neither would speak to the other without wittiness present. The stress became too much for Joe Brandt, who said he would sell out to the first brother to give him $500,000 for his share of the business.

Both brothers tried to raise the cash. However, it was in the midst of the Depression and the banks weren't lending, so Harry Cohn turned to Johnny Roselli for help. Roselli put Cohn in touch with New Jersey rackets boss Longy Zwillman, who was worth millions in cold, hard cash. Zwillman, who had deep interests in Hollywood, loaned Cohn the money to buy Brandt, no doubt taking his pound of flesh in return.

Cohn returned the favor to Roselli in 1937 when the hood had an opportunity to buy into the Santa Anita racetrack with Bugsy Siegel for $20,000. Cohn gave Roselli the money to make the deal and, several months later, when Roselli gave Cohn a check for the $20,000 he borrowed, plus interest, Cohn refused to take the interest money, and insisted that Roselli rewrite the check just for the balance owed. Roselli took the difference, and, reverting to an Old Italian custom, purchased two matching rings, star rubies in gold, which would symbolize their friendship for life. Roselli wore one and gave the other to Cohn who wore it with pride.

When Roselli was locked away for his role in the Bioff scandal his name became poison in Hollywood. After his release from prison, Cohn, like so many other people in the business, didn't want anything to do with Johnny Roselli, in fact, when Roselli needed Cohn to put him on the payroll so he could get parole, Cohn refused, claiming that the studio's investors would balk.

Roselli was stunned and hurt, and swore his revenge.

Now, using the Sinatra business as his excuse, Roselli would have his revenge. In a tense meeting in Cohn's office, Roselli reportedly ordered Cohn to give Sinatra the part of Angelo Maggio in the film. Cohn not only refused, he told Roselli, "John, if we have a problem here, I'm going to have to make some phone calls," referring to Cohn's own considerable contact in the underworld.

But Roselli had the backing of the entire national syndicate behind him and knew that Cohn was defenseless. "Harry," he said, "If we have a problem here, you're a fucking dead man." In the end Sinatra got the part and the Academy Award as well.

*****

Cohen-Dragna War: Micky Cohen, born Cohen Meyer Harris Born September 4, 1913 Brooklyn, New York. Died July 29 1976. Mickey Cohen was an affable, if slightly mentally unbalanced drug pusher in LA, by way of Chicago. Jack Dragna represented the local LA Mafia, the so-called Micky Mouse Mob.

   Originally from Brooklyn, the Cohen's moved to Los Angeles in 1920, where Micky's father ran a drug store. At the start of prohibition, Cohen's older made gin in the back of the store at Micky, at age 9, was the operations delivery boy until he was arrested.

   Cohen turned to prize fighting in his teen years and had a brief but respectable career before he landed in Chicago and worked in the Capone organization at various odd jobs but was forced to leave town after he took part in a gun battle that left several gamblers dead.

Cleveland mobster Lou Rothkopf is said to have taken a liking to Cohen, something that was easy to do, and sent him to Los Angeles to work with Bugsy Siegel. When Siegel was murdered in 1947, Cohen was granted most of the dead gangsters gambling operations around Los Angeles.

Rothkopf

It was around this time that Cohen supposedly Cohen introduced a hoodlum named Johnny Stompanato to troubled movie starlet Lana Turner. Cohen then wired Stompanato's bedroom and recorded the actress and Stompanato having sex and then pressed two thousand copies of the master recording and sold them $5 each. Turner's daughter, Cheryl, later stabbed Stompanato to death in a killing ruled to be justifiable homicide.

The essence of the Dragna-Cohen war was control and power. Although Dragna was the unquestioned Mafia power west of Las Vegas, he felt slighted within the ranks of the traditional mob that moved in on Las Vegas without so much as a nod to him and generally disrespected by freelance hoods like Mickey Cohen and Jack Whalen who ran their bookie and narcotics operations.

Dragna and Cohen could not be more different. Jack Dragna (He was born Ignazio Dragna but renamed himself years later in LA) was born on April 18, 1891, in Corleone, Sicily and arrived in the United States as a child. He returned to Sicily in 1908 and served a hitch in the Italian army. He then travelled back to the US in 1914. Dragna is the suspected killer of Bernard Baff, a hapless kosher chicken wholesaler in Brooklyn. There is a possibility that Dragna worked with the New York mobs and the Capone operation at some point before venturing out west. Over the years, he had convictions for attempted extortion (1915) and served time in San Quinton prison. He was released in 1918 and never again arrested for a serious offense.

Dragna, who lived at 3927 Hubert Avenue in Los Angeles, took over the tiny LA outfit in 1931 after the boss, Joe Ardizonne vanished in 1931. (He lived at 10949 North Mount Gleason Avenue) A shy and retiring person, he avoided the limelight and the newspaper people. However, on April 15, 1951, when the LA police began a harassment campaign against the Mafia, the cops recorded Dragna having sex in his girlfriend's trailer at 330 Mariposa Street in LA and arrested him (and her) for engaging in lewd acts by consent (Oral sex)

Mickey Cohen, on the other hand, went out of his way to bring attention to himself, especially the press, which generally went lightly on him as a flashy, interesting character. Flashy, good humored and outgoing, Cohen quickly became the overall public favorite in the short lived, almost comical war with Dragna largely because Cohen understood the fundamentals of public relations. When an elderly widow named Elsie Phillips lost her house at 5631 Homeside Avenue in LA in a suit over an unpaid $8.00 radio repair bill, Cohen paid the lien judgment ($1,013.95) for her. Then his men beat the radio repairman up.

The shooting started when Dragna demanded a piece of the $40 per phone per week plus a general surcharge of $5.00 that Cohen was charging bookie. Cohen refused. So on February 7, 1950, Dragna, planted a bomb under Cohen's home on 413 Moreno Blvd. in West Hollywood. (The same street where Jack Dragna lived)

The bomb, which went off at 4:15 AM, left a crater ten feet deep and broke every window in every house for 5,000 feet around. The explosion was felt seven miles away. The problem was, for Dragna anyway, was that his men had placed the bomb directly under a double laid cement floor where Cohen kept his safe. Because of that, the bomb blasted sideways instead of upwards. All that happened to Cohen was that the explosion lifted him up out of his bed and threw him back down again. His wife, LaVonne, their maid and the Cohen family dog were uninjured in the blast.

Members of the Sica gang were rounded up and questioned in the bombing but released when no evidence could be found to tie them to the case.

"I am completely in the dark as to who done it" Cohen said and then added "And I ain't no gangster" The newspapers reported that Cohen was "almost put to tears" that his neighbors could have been hurt in the blast. One neighbor responded "That's very touching. What would be even more touching is if Cohen moved away from here" The neighbors then declared the Cohen "an intolerable nuisance" and demanded they leave the neighborhood. Cohen sent out a three- page letter to each resident, begging their forgiveness and asking that they reconsider.

Next, Dragna sent Sam Bruno to shot Cohen to death. Bruno was said to be the best shot in the mob. One bright, beautiful afternoon he hid behind a tree and fired a shotgun into Cohen's car as he drove by. He fired another round and effectively killed the car but Cohen was untouched. The bullets didn't even come near him.

After that, mobster started saying, and probably believing, that Cohen made a pack with the devil. In Las Vegas, they were actually taking odds on how long it would take to kill him off and the odds were in Micky Cohen's favor. There were a number of failed attempts, all of which Cohen survived, basically through dumb luck.

The Kefauver Committee caused Cohen to be convicted of income tax evasion. He was sentenced to four years in federal prison. In 1961, a separate indictment found him guilty of income tax evasion in a second case. Sent to Alcatraz, Cohen was attacked by another inmate who hit the aging gangster in the skull with a lead pipe, dramatically affecting his motor skills.

"The guy" Cohen said "scrambled my brains" He was released from prison in 1972 and died in his sleep four years later.

*****

Colorado Mob: Pete and Sam Carlino established the Mafia in southern Colorado in 1930 when they made their push to expand their bootlegging into the Denver area. Joe Roma, (AKA"Little Caesar" due to his five-foot-one stature) the boss of Denver, agreed to a meeting the brothers in an effort to head off a gang war. On January 24, 1931, Roma and at least 30 of Colorado's top bootleggers sat down to talk. However, police raided the meeting. The Carlino's saw a set up and declared war. On February 18, 1930, Pete Carlino was shot by gunmen from a passing automobile as he walked down a street. He survived but afterwards, Sam Carlino and James Colletti, a lieutenant, was killed at Carlino's home. The Carlino gang accused Bruno Mauro of Pueblo as the killer. On September 10-11, 1931, Pete Carlino was murdered while driving to Canon City to visit a cousin. He body was stuffed beneath a bridge. When no one discovered the body, the shooters returned and moved the body to a place where it could be more easily discovered. Roma continued to rule over southern Colorado until his murder on February 18, 1933.

*****

Conrad Robert: The Chicago born film actor was a guest at the wedding of Tony Accardo's granddaughter, Alicia, when she married in a top rate ceremony at the Hilton Hotel in Chicago. Alicia once worked for Conrad in Hollywood

*****

Dalitz, Morris Barney: Casino owner. AKA Moe. Born December 24, 1899 Boston, Massachusetts. Died August. 31, 1989. The son of Barney Dalitz a gambler and prosperous industrial laundry business operator in Ann Arbor, Dalitz used his family trucks to bring thousands of cases of whisky across the Canadian border and into the US. His gang, at first it was actually more of collection of vaguely competent young men hoping to pass as gangsters, was called the Mayfield Road Boys. Mayfield Road being the point where Cleveland ended at the shores of Lake Erie. The gang operated between Cleveland, Detroit, and Ann Arbor. It was during this time that Dalitz met a very young Jimmy Hoffa, also from Michigan. Hoffa had tried (but failed) to unionize Dalitz's laundry drivers

He served in the US Army in World War 2, achieving the rank of Captain. Pressure from the Kefauver hearings and requests by the Mafia moved Dalitz to Las Vegas, although he had been operating there, as a consultant of sorts, to the Mafia, since the 1940s. The move was simply a formality. Dalitz took over construction of the troubled Desert Inn Casino from builder Wilbur Clark who had run out money. Dalitz with his partners, the ethically challenged Sam Tucker and Morris Kleinman, Dalitz opened the hotel in 1950. In 1954, he took over the Stardust Hotel after the questionable sudden death of its builder, LA gangster Tony Cornero.

Wilbur Clark

Unlike virtually everyone around him, muscle and violence were not the way Dalitz handled problems. Crime writer Hank Messick said "The reaction of Dalitz to a threat was typical of the man and of his methods. Even in those pioneering days of rum running across Lake Erie, Dalitz and his associates used others to do the dirty work.

Building the Desert Inn

Caution, not fear, was the basis of their method of operation. Even as young men, they understood the value of insulation, of remaining apart from physical violence. A fellow with brains and cash could always find a man with muscle to man the 'rummies,' as the boats carrying illicit booze were known. If necessary, they could also do a little killing." That attitude "Think first, shoot later" permeated across Las Vegas where, by general agreement of the mobs, violence could happen, but it was rare. Yet it was Dalitz, in his capacity as advisor to the National Mafia Commission on all things Las Vegas, who pushed for Bugsy Siegel's death. According to Chicago's capo, Murray Humphreys, who had hired Dalitz to consult on Vegas, Dalitz advocated Siegel's murder because Bugsy would never stand for being pushed out of Nevada. He would simply come back looking for a war.

His wealth was estimated to be in the area of $100 million and most of that was made through shrewd real estate investment deal in California and investments in the television entertainment industry. Despite his millions, or maybe because of his millions, Dalitz could be seen around Vegas driving a yellow Volkswagen Beatle and wearing clothes that most suspected were purchased at low-end retail outlets. He was expressly proud of his Jewish background and contributed liberally to Jewish causes (He also gave millions to the University of Nevada, Las Vegas) Dalitz continued to be a major power in Las Vegas and Nevada well after he retired. He died of natural causes, rare for an originator of the Las Vegas dream and is one of the few legendary figures of organized crime of whom it can be correctly written was never convicted of a major crime.

*****

Vegas 1972

Dallas Mob: In the late 1950s, Frank Tortoriello was identified by the FBI as a member of the Dallas Mafia and a partner with mobster Joe Campisi in several enterprises. Both Tortoriello and Campisi were suspected of answering to the New Orleans Mafia but no definite connection has ever been established. On November 20, 1963, Jack Ruby, who assassinated Lee Harvey Oswald, was with Tortoriello at the Tanglewood apartments in Dallas with a stripper named Jada who worked in Ruby's clubs. The Dallas mob no longer exists. What role, if any, Campisi played in the Kennedy-Oswald murders, is unknown.

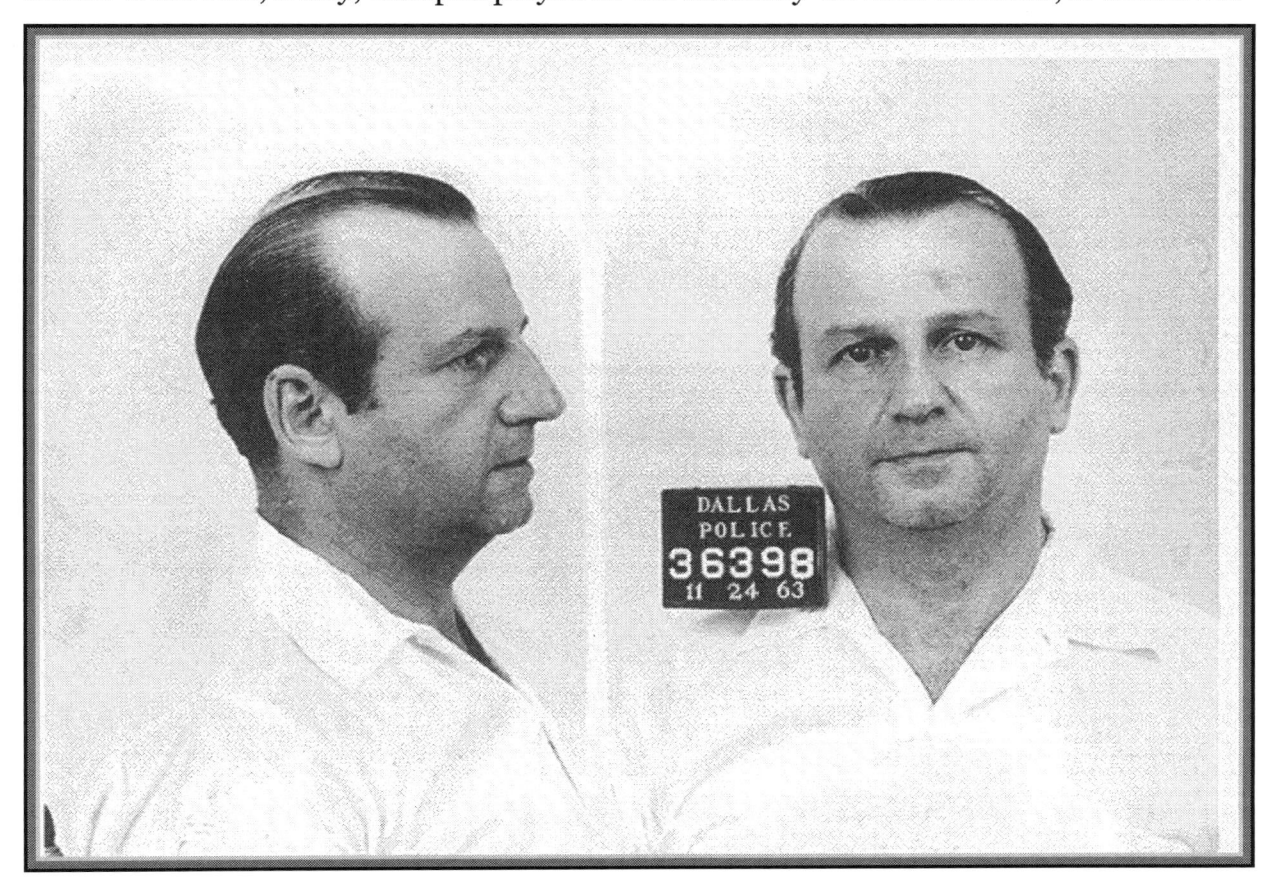

Jack Ruby, whose underworld contacts, especially in Chicago, were extensive

*****

DeSimone Frank: A criminal attorney, DeSimone (Uncle of Goodfellas character Tommy DeSimone)

Tommy DeSimone

In 1957, he replaced Jack Dragna after Dragna's death, becoming the second DeSimone family descendant to become Los Angeles don. DeSimone was later disbarred and died of a heart attack on August 4th 1967. He thought to be the inspiration for the Robert Duvall character Tom Hagen in the 1972 film The Godfather, although DeSimone was far less civil than the fictional Hagan.

Tommy DeSimone

On June 18, 1956, right after he took over, his Underboss, Girolomo "Momo" Adamo, committed suicide in San Diego after seriously wounding his wife over an affair she was having with DeSimone. It turned out, they had not had an affair but that DeSimone had raped her and warned her not to talk. Basically DeSimone was a junior partner and go-fer for the New York and Chicago Families but he powerful enough to be present at the Apalachin Conference. DeSimone lived in fear that he was going to be assassinated and, oddly enough, Boss Joe Bonanno did plan to have him killed in his push to take over the Five Families. DeSimone died in 1968 and was succeeded by Nicholas Licata.

*****

DeSimone, Rosario: Boss of Los Angeles, San Diego and Las Vegas from 1931 until his death in 1946. He was a distant relative of Tommy DeSimone, a real life character portrayed in the film Goodfellas.

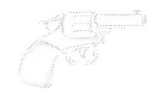

*****

Entratter, Jack: Onetime doorman-bouncer at the Stork Club in Manhattan before moving over to the Copacabana. Myer Lansky's Mafia protector, Jimmy "Blue Eyes" Alo offered him a job in Vegas overlooking the Sands Casino with a 12- point interest in the place, or at least on the books. In all probability Entratter was a placeholder for Mafia bosses.

*****

Epstein, Joe: AKA Joey Ep. Born 1902. Lived at the Saint Claire Hotel, Chicago and 162 East Ohio Street, Chicago. An accountant/Book keeper for the Mob for many decades, his essential job was to launder cash for the Outfit. He was a business partner of Lenny Patrick of the so-called "Jewish arm" of the mob that once operated in the Rogers Park section. He was also romantically involved with Bugsy Siegel's girlfriend Virginia Hill and kept her supplied with cash for decades.

Hill, a foul-mouthed, tough-talking product of the poverty, had arrived in Chicago from rural Bessemer Alabama at age 17 in 1933 to work at the Century of Progress Exhibition. She tried a variety of jobs, waitressing, short order cook, (including a stint as a shimmy dancer for $20 a week, very good money at the time) but finally became a street walker. Hill was a beautiful young woman and was soon taken in by the Fischetti brothers and more or less, adopted by Jake Guzik and his bisexual wife, who offered to put her in charge of several brothels they still owned, but Virginia turned them down. She said she had higher aspirations. The Fischetti's gave her a job as a waitress/ prostitute at their casino, the Colony Club. Other owners in the club included Nick Circella (alias Nick Dean) who was later implicated in the million-dollar movie-extortion Bioff case. Circella's brother August Circella, ran the club. August had run a series of casinos across Chicago including the Gold Coast Lounge, on North Rush Street. In later years, August would grow rich when he purchased the patent rights for a window unit air conditioner. It was here that she met the bespectacled and withdrawn Joey Ep, a man who barely spoke to those around him. Nevertheless, he was dependable and honest, by mob standards, and had been Guzik's understudy since 1930 and would one day be his second-in-command.

Epp ran the outfit's racetracks with such authority the newspapers called him Illinois' unofficial racetrack commissioner. And while Epstein was well read, some said an intellectual, he loved to party and he was fascinated by the lowlife around him. He fell head over heels in love with Virginia Hill, and put her on the payroll as his mistress.

But it was a working relationship as well. Epstein put Virginia to work as a courier, bringing suitcases full of the mob's dirty money from Chicago, Kansas City, Cleveland and Los Angeles to syndicate owned and run banks in Cuba, Mexico, the Dominican Republic, France and Switzerland. There, the money was laundered, usually at a price of ten cents on a dollar and then invested in legitimate business from which the hoods could draw a salary.

The second part of the plan called for Virginia to get in touch with Bugsy Siegel, which she did, having met, and romanced him, several times in the past. Like Joey Epp before him, Bugsy Siegel fell head over heels in love with Virginia. He called her his "Flamingo" and drenched her in jewelry, furs and gowns.

When the Gangster Chronicles came on television in the late 1970's, a relative of Bugsy Siegel remarked to Meyer Lansky, Siegel's lifelong business partner, that he was considering suing the production company for depicting Bugsy as an uncontrollable killer.

"What are you going to sue them for?" asked Lansky. "In real life he was worse."

Unlike most hoods who dominated gangdom in the 1930's, Siegel was smart and he knew it. He hated the poverty and ignorance of the world he was raised in and detested the illiterate and uncouth men he had to deal with. He wanted more, he wanted to be on the other side. In fact, Siegel wanted to be on the other side, the legitimate side, so badly, that he invested a million dollars in the stock market in 1933, but lost half of it when the market crashed in October. "If I had kept that million," he said, "I'd have been out of the rackets right now."

Siegel knew that if he stayed in New York, nothing would ever change, so he, and not the New York branch of the syndicate as is commonly reported, decided to try his luck out west in Los Angeles. He had been a regular visitor out there since 1933, introducing himself as an independent sportsman, a title that didn't fool anybody.

Of course, Bugsy had other motives. Gangsters always do. He had stabbed another hood in a dispute over a card game, cutting the man in the stomach 20 times to make sure gases would not allow his body to float to the surface, and now the cops wanted to talk to him about that. He had also been named in a scam to fix boxing matches and had ordered the killing of a bookie that had cheated him. When the bookie found out about the death order, he went to the cops and told them everything he knew, so for the time being it was best he went to the West Coast.

Siegel took over the Screen Extras Guild and the Los Angeles Teamsters, which he ran until his death. With control of the Screen Extras Guild, Siegel was able to shake down Warner Brothers Studios for $10,000, with a refusal to provide extras for any of their films. He also shook down his movie star friends for huge loans that he never paid back, and when he came back for another loan, he always got it, because they were, justifiably, terrified of him.

He once bragged to Lansky that he had fleeced the Hollywood crowd out of more than $400,000 within six months of his arrival. He was a one man terrorist campaign.

When Siegel arrived in LA, the number one racing service out west was James Ragen's Continental Press, which serviced thousands of bookies between Chicago to Los Angeles, each of whom paid Ragen $100 to $1200. The owner, Jimmy Ragen, was a tough, two fisted, Chicago born Irishman, who had punched, stabbed, and shot his way to the top of the heap, without the Mob's help.

The Chicago outfit, then under Nitti, watched the money flood into Regan's office with envy. Nitti, and later Paul Ricca, tried to set up a rival service called Trans-American, with each mob boss across the country running the local outlet, doing whatever they had to do to take Ragen out of business.

In California, Siegel and Mafiosi Jack Dragna were charged with putting Trans-America in business and taking Ragen's Continental Press out of business. Eventually, the Chicago mob settled the entire issue by shooting Ragen as he drove his car down a Chicago street. Ragen survived the shooting, but not the dose of mercury a nurse working for the outfit shot up into his vein a few days later. With Ragen dead, Continental Racing Services was divided up among the various bosses who had helped to build it, and Jack Dragna was named to run the California office. Siegel was shocked. He had risked his life to build the service out west, he had worked on it day and night, at the least he expected to be cut in on perhaps half the franchise.

Instead, all he was got was a visit from Chicago's chief fixer, Murray Humphreys, who told Siegel to fold up Trans-America wire service. They didn't need it anymore. The syndicate owned Continental Press. But Siegel sent Humphreys packing with a message for Paul Ricca... if the Chicago people wanted Siegel to fold up Trans-America in Nevada, Arizona and Southern California, it would cost them $2,000,000 in cash.

Jack Dragna, 1968 (Above) and 1915 (Below)

Even though the Chicago outfit didn't want Siegel working for them, at the same time, they didn't want him working for New York either. Crazy or not, Siegel was smart, ambitious and ruthless. They had to watch him, so Paul Ricca told Charlie Fischetti, one of his most dependable torpedoes, to send out a spy, and the woman they chose was the same woman Bugsy Siegel came to call his Flamingo, Virginia Hill.

Virginia reported every conversation she had with Siegel back to the Fischetti brothers in Chicago. Still, the boys back in Chicago never trusted Hill, or anyone else for that matter, and when Paul Ricca came to power, he told Johnny Roselli to start an affair with Hill so he could keep tabs on her.

Then, Siegel watched a colorful Los Angeles hood named Tony Cornero move his entire gambling organization out of California and into Nevada where he and his brothers opened a rundown but very profitable casino on the Vegas Strip. Within a year, Siegel had the cash, most of it from the New York end of the syndicate, to build the fabulous Flamingo Hotel.

In May of 1947, one month before he was executed, Bugsy Siegel called Jimmy Fratianno, a Los Angeles hood who, technically anyway, worked for Chicago, and asked him to come out to Las Vegas for a meeting. He didn't tell them what it concerned, but, as they found out, it was a recruitment drive. He had already made the same pitch to Jack Dragna, Bugsy Siegel was planning the unheard of, and he was going to start his own organization out in the Nevada desert.

Virginia Hill had already reported Siegel's plans to Paul Ricca in Chicago, and, even though the Chicago mob was chiseling Siegel in the Flamingo by sending in professional gamblers to break the bank, they were indignant. As far as they were concerned, although the syndicate had agreed to allow Vegas and Reno to operate as open cities, it was clearly understood in the syndicate that Chicago controlled everything west of the Mississippi.

Siegel was a regional problem at a time when the mob thought it had gotten over its regional misunderstandings. He was a relic from the past. He had to be removed.

On June 8, 1947, Virginia Hill got a call from Epstein back in Chicago, he told her to get out of town, to go to France, and she could tell Siegel she was going there to buy wine for the casino as she had in the past. He wouldn't question that. Virginia knew, immediately, why she had to leave town. They were going to kill Bugsy and the boys back in Chicago didn't want their best cash courier and narcotics peddler splattered with blood and headlines. Virginia flew into Chicago and met Epstein at Midway airport, where he gave her $5,000 and then she continued to Paris.

Back on the West Coast, Bugsy Siegel, caught in the middle of an uprising, was too busy to care where Virginia was. Several days before, Siegel told Micky Cohen to tell all of the bookies in Los Angeles, Reno and Vegas that the price for using the wire service was going to double. But, to Siegel's amazement, the bookies refused to pay, they knew that Chicago was taking over and that they were planning to kill Siegel.

And, on June 20, 1947, that's what they did.

Jack Dragna gave the order to a hood named Frankie Carranzo. When the call came, Carranzo drove up to Beverly Hills and parked his car a few feet from Siegel's home, wound the silencer onto the barrel of his .30 caliber, army issue carbine, and walked around to the back of the house. He hid in the shadow of a rose-covered lattice work with his army carbine and released an entire clip into the living room through a 14-inch pane of glass.

Nine slugs in all. Two of them tore apart Bugsy's face as he sat on a chintz-covered couch. One bullet smashed the bridge of his nose and drove into his left eye. The eye was later found on the dining room floor, fifteen feet away from his dead body. The bullet was found in an English painting on the wall. The other entered his right cheek, passed through the back of his neck, and shattered a vertebra, ripped across the room.

At exactly 11:00 A.M., Jack Dragna got a call from Carranzo: "The insect was killed," and he then hung up.

A few minutes before that call, at 10:55, Little Moe Sedway and Gus Greenbaum, two hoods with gambling backgrounds, strode into the Flamingo and announced over the intercom system, "OK, we're taking over."

Everyone present knew who "we" were.

The only persons to attend Siegel's funeral services at Beth Olam Cemetery were his brother and a Rabbi.

Virginia Hill continued working for the Chicago outfit as a courier for several more years before they replaced her in 1950. She married a guy who wasn't involved with the outfit and had a child, but that ended in divorce.

Joey Epp never fell out of love with her, and he kept her on the books for as long as they bosses would let him, but eventually even that stopped.

In the 1950s when investigators followed a cash trail from Epstein to Hill, the gun moll was questioned about it by US Senator Charles Tobey who asked "But why would Joe Epstein give you money Miss Hill?" to which Hill replied "You really want to know?"
"Yes, I do" said Tobey
"The" replied Hill "I'll tell you why. Because I'm the best cocksucker in town"

When the cash did stop coming in, it was widely rumored in gangland that Virginia, desperate for cash, started to extort money out of Joe Adonis and other mob guys for whom she had carried narcotics over the years. On March 24, 1966, near a brook in Koppl Austria, a small town near Salzburg, two hikers found Virginia Hill's dead body. Austrian officials, not understanding who Hill had been, ruled her unusual death a suicide by poison.

   The Flamingo's next manager was Gus Greenbaum. He did his job. The hotel was completed and enlarged from 97 to two hundred rooms. By the end of the year the casino posted a $4 million profit, $15 million before the skim, clearing the way for the skimming to begin.

*****

The LAPD "Gangster Squad" of the early 1950s. Their job was to keep the Mob from gaining a foothold in LA. Their methods were simple. When new hoods arrived in the city, they were arrested the hoods for vagrancy, beaten up jailed, beaten up and tossed out of the city. It worked. The mob never took a toehold in LA beyond a small presence.

Giancana, the Kennedy, and Sinatra: In September of 1933, Joe Kennedy secured the representation for Gordon's Dry Gin, Haig & Haig and Dewers. He set up his distributorship, Somerset Importers, with the relatively small investment of $100,000. Within a short time, the franchises were bringing Kennedy $250,000.00 a year. Kennedy's southern representative in the business was Charlie Block who was in a separate partnership with Miami gambler, Bert Wingy Grober who was also a friend of Kennedy's. That connection proved helpful in 1944, when Kennedy was having a problem breaking his Haig & Haig whisky into the Chicago market. Kennedy asked Block to put him in contact with Grober who in turn placed Kennedy in to touch with Tom Cassara, a Miami Beach mobster.

Giancana, circa 1950

One of Cassara's business partners was Chicago gangster Rocco DeStefano. With DeStefano help, Cassara was able to work a distribution deal for himself with the Chicago Mobs representative, Joey Fusco. Fusco had been one of Al Capone's most reliable bootleggers and had begun his career as Diamond Joe Esposito right hand man and go between for Esposito and the Genna brother's gang during the prohibition. In 1931 the Chicago Crime Commission briefly named Fusco public enemy number one.

Joe Kennedy knew Fusco already because he had been a friend with Fusco boss, Diamond Joe Esposito during the prohibition. Before he was gunned on Johnny Torrio's order, Esposito took credit for saving Kennedy's life, claiming that Old Joe had come to him for help because the Purple Gang, Detroit's vicious criminal organization, had placed a contract on his life for bringing bootleg rum into their empire without their permission or paying the usual tribute paid to them. Esposito bragged that Kennedy begged him to call to ask the Purple gang to call off the contract on his life. Esposito said he did and supposedly, thereafter Kennedy was in debt to the Chicago Organization.

The story doesn't sound like it has much merit and it although it may be based in some truth; overall, its facts are very questionable. However, Joe Fusco traveled in the same company with Murray Humphreys, and Chicago's Mafia Don's Paul Ricca and Tony Accardo and was a minor owner, off the books, in the Sands Casino in Las Vegas with two other friends of Joe Kennedy's, Frank Sinatra and Joe Doc Starcher. (1902-1977) (Starcher was later deported out of the US on Bobby Kennedy's orders. Starcher claimed it was Joe Kennedy having his revenge. It's more likely that fate, the Justice Department and a snitch, caught up with him)

Doc Starcher (Above)

In the summer of 1946, Tom Cassara, the small time Miami Beach gambler, stupidly sensed that he could become Kennedy's partner if he could force Joe Fusco out of the picture and distribute Kennedy's booze in Chicago without a mob tribute, and started talking tough to Fusco. One night Casara was called into the Trade Winds Bar and Restaurant on Rush Street. The bars' owners were two former 42 gang members, Marshal Caifano and Sam "Teets" Battaglia. Cassara was shot in the head, and was found outside of the restaurant, laying in the gutter. He recovered, said he didn't know how he got shot, and moved to Los Angles where he was known to be a mob front man for Chicago in its real estate dealings.

According to Johnny Roselli, Tony Accardo never bought Casara's story that he was acting on his own. The Big Tuna figured that Joe Kennedy had duped Casara into trying to bluff the Chicago. On July 31, 1946, Joe Kennedy suddenly and unexpectedly sold his Whiskey import business to a firm owned by New Jersey rackets boss Longy Zwillman and his partner Joe Reinfield for a reported paltry $8,000,000 (Reinfield is still in business) Kennedy always insisted that he got out of the extremely lucrative import business because he had high intentions for his son's political career, and owning a liqueur business might hurt him in the more conservative states. However, for decades, Joe Fusco insisted that the Chicago Mob, which, Fusco said, put up most of the cash for Zwillman and Reinfield to buy Somerset, forced Kennedy out.

Elmer "Bones" Renner was an old-time gangster from San Francisco who owned the Cal-Neva lodge and Casino at Crystal Bay on the Nevada side of Lake Tahoe. He also owed the IRS $800,000.00 in back taxes, and so, on paper anyway, ownership of the Cal-Neva passed to another old time hood named Bert "Wingy" Grober, who also, as a result of his sudden and unexplainable ownership of a casino, ended up with his own set of tax problems. With the IRS after him, Grober placed the Cal-Neva up for sale.

On July 13, 1960, the day Kennedy won the democratic nomination in Los Angeles, it was announced to the newspapers that Frank Sinatra, Dean Martin, Hank Sincola, a Sinatra pal and business partner, and Skinny D'Amato, a convicted white slaver, had applied for permission from the state of Nevada to take over the lodge. What didn't make the papers about the deal was that Sam Giancana and the Chicago outfit owned a secret percentage in the Cal-Neva and that it was Giancana's influence that persuaded Wingy Grober to sell the place off for the extremely reasonable price of $250,000.00. What also didn't make the newspapers about the deal was the FBI assumption that Sinatra was nothing more than a front in the Cal-Neva for New York's mob boss Anthony "Fat Tony" Salerno.

Sinatra had been around the Mob for a while. In 1939, an unknown but talented crooner named Albert Francis Sinatra left the working, poor, Italian neighborhoods of Hoboken, New Jersey and signed an exclusive performance agreement with the popular Tommy Dorsey Band. Under the terms of the contract, which was written by Dorsey himself, the band leader took an incredible 33% of all of Sinatra's earnings. Dorsey's manager, Lenny Vannerson, took an additional 10%, and Sinatra's own agent took another 10%. In all, 53% of the young man's earnings were gone before taxes and expenses. Union memberships took another 30%. It was so bad for Sinatra financially that he was forced to borrow money to buy a suit to make his stage appearances. Over the next few months, as his popularity grew, Sinatra spent thousands of dollars on lawyers' fees to find ways to break the deal, but Dorsey had twice Sinatra's money and a legal fight would have dragged on for years. The young singer went to the artist unions for help, but they were useless. Tommy Dorsey was a very powerful man in the entertainment business. The national depression was still lingering and thousands of professional musicians were out of work. The unions had struck profitable deals with Dorsey, and they were not about to jeopardize those agreements for an unknown kid from New Jersey who might end up tomorrow's has been.

According to Sinatra, after the unions let him down, he took his troubles to Jules Stein, the powerful and very mobbed up Chicagoan who had founded MCA, the world's biggest theatrical agency. Remarkably, Stein was able to secure Sinatra's release for $60,000, in cash, an enormous amount of money in the 1940s, and certainly far more than the $500 that Dorsey was taking out of Sinatra's weekly pay for expenses. In later years, Dorsey explained the agreement with Stein, by saying that from a business standpoint, it was a smart deal, because he wasn't sure how long the singer would stay on top of the popularity heap. The way Dorsey saw it; he had been around long enough to know that in the popular music business, one month is an eternity. Two years was impossibility. Furthermore, kids, who were Sinatra's primary fans, were fickle. Loyalties and followings changed overnight. Dorsey was sure Sinatra was a flash in the pan. Dorsey said he wasn't happy with Sinatra anyway. Stories about the married Sinatra's eye for women were starting to show up in small pieces in the press. That sort of thing didn't happen in the forties. At least not in public. Nor was Dorsey pleased with Sinatra's ongoing spats with his drummer Buddy Rich. The stage wasn't big enough for both of their egos, and that's what it was all about, really. Ego. Sinatra had taken the spotlight away from Tommy Dorsey. As one of the band members remarked, "It wasn't Tommy's show anymore, it was Frank's." Dorsey thought it was his band that had made Sinatra the sensation that he was, and once Dorsey let him go, Sinatra's star would just fade away. That was Dorsey's version of what happened. Another version, now part of popular lore, was that for several months Dorsey refused the $60,000 that Jules Stein had offered him to release Sinatra from his contract, simply because Dorsey had grown to despise Sinatra and intended to hold on to his contract and drive the singer's career into the ground, which he could easily do by simply keeping him off stage and radio. But, Sinatra's strong willed and politically connected mother went to see New Jersey's Mafia boss, Quarico Moretti, better known as Willie Moretti, who controlled large parts of the East Coast entertainment industry. In fact, by the early 1940s, the national syndicate still held a virtual lock on the entertainment business unions nationwide and Mobsters were always looking to expand their control of the industry by managing the careers of promising entertainers.

Moretti saw that Sinatra's prospects were good, and agreed to get the young man released from his contract with Dorsey for a cash payment from Sinatra, plus a percentage of his future earnings. Working through Jules Stein, Moretti's first offer to Dorsey was $60,000 cash. When Dorsey turned that down, Moretti, who was considered, in mob circles, to be a madman, decided to take matters into his own hands, and make the band leader an offer he couldn't refuse. One night after a show, Moretti pushed his way into Dorsey's dressing room, put a gun in the band leader's mouth and told Dorsey to sell Sinatra's contract. Which he did. For one dollar. As for the $60,000 paid by MCA to release Sinatra, supposedly that money, in cash, went directly from Dorsey's bank account into Moretti's greedy little hands, after Dorsey paid the taxes on it. Sinatra always denied the story too, and claimed he barely knew Moretti, who lived only a few doors away from him in suburban New Jersey. Dorsey spent the rest of his life denying the gun in the mouth story, but in 1951, right after Moretti was killed, Dorsey only added credence to the tale, when he told American Mercury Magazine that he signed the contract releasing Sinatra because one night, three men paid him in his dressing room, placed Sinatra's release in front of him and said, "Sign it or else!"

When the National syndicate held its conclave in Cuba in the 1940s, the Fischetti brothers were there with Frank Sinatra. (1915-1998) Sinatra later explained that he wasn't aware that the Fischetti's were gangsters and that he had first met them in Chicago during a benefit at the Chez Paree, a night club owned and managed by the Mob. The Fischetti's, Sinatra claimed, were star struck and insisted Sinatra use their cars and boats while he was in town and from that a friendship developed. In early January of 1947, Rocca Fischetti called Sinatra and asked him to join him down in Havana. Sinatra agreed and on January 13 1947 Sinatra requested a gun permit, saying that he sometimes carried large sums of money and needed the gun for protection. Sinatra flew to New York and then to Miami where he stayed at Charlie Fischetti mansion.

The night before leaving for Havana, Sinatra and Joe Fischetti were spotted in the Colonial Inn, the casino in Hallendale owned by Frank Costello (1891-1973) and New Jersey boss Joe Adonis (Born Joe Doto 1902-1972) and Meyer Lansky where Sinatra put on a free concert. On February 11, 1947, Sinatra and the Fischetti's were photographed walking down the steps of a Pan American clipper at the Havana airport. They checked into Meyer Lansky's Hotel, the Nacional, where 36 suites had been reserved for the Mob bosses which included Albert Anastasia, (1903-1957) Carlo Gambino, Willie Moretti, (1894-1951) Vito Genovese, (1897-1969) Frank Costello, Augie Pisano (? -1959) Joe Fat Man Magliocco, (1898-1963) Joe Bonanno, Tommy Three finger Brown Lucchese, (circa1900-1967) Joe Profaci, Joe Adonis Tony Accardo, Sam Giancana, (1908-1975) Carlo Marcello, (1910-1993) Dandy Phil Kastel, Santo Trafficante and Meyer Lansky and Jospeh Doc Stacher who now controlled Lansky Juke boxes and slot machines in Jersey City.

Sinatra wasn't in the mob meeting, in Havana, but he was in the hotel. The singer had arrived in Havana, by plane, with the Fischetti brothers. Another story that made the rounds, then and now and later portrayed in the film, The Godfather, was that Rocco Fischetti had several travel bags stuffed with two million dollars, the proceeds from narcotics sales that was owed to Lucky Luciano. (1897-1962)

Rocco Fischetti

 Terrified that he would be stopped and searched as he left the United States, Fischetti had brought Sinatra along to carry the bags into Cuba, were tailing him. Traditionally, star struck customs agents didn't check celebrity's baggage. Actually, a writer named Lee Mortimer (Born in Chicago as Mortimer Lieberman in 1906) spread the money in the suit case story. Mortimer disliked Sinatra intensely and at one time the dispute brought the two men to blows. The FBI added to Mortimer's story. Sinatra denied the story saying "if you can show me how to get two million dollars into a briefcase, I'll give you the two million dollars"

The fact is the syndicate didn't need Frank Sinatra to lug around its dope proceeds for them. They had worked out a transportation system years ago thanks to the genius of Meyer Lansky. If they had to lug it across the country, as Sam Giancana said later "Sinatra is the last guy you would use for that. He would draw attention. When you transport money you always use a woman with a child or a grandmotherly type. Not movie stars" As for Giancana's interest in the money-losing casino, he was probably only in the deal to keep next to Sinatra, who was trying, desperately, to keep next to Kennedy, which everybody in the Chicago outfit wanted. Before the deal was signed, Dean Martin saw the mob's interests in the casino and pulled out of the deal. Sinatra was convinced that the Cal-Neva, a seasonal place, could be turned around, that it could produce a hefty profit, even with the mob connected pit bosses stealing the place blind, and he told Giancana that with the right investment the place could become a year-round operation. To draw attention to the place, on opening night, Sinatra's personality guests included Marilyn Monroe, Joe Kennedy, and his son John. Also there that weekend was Johnny Roselli and Sam Giancana. Uninvited and hiding up in the hills around the casino lodge, was Hoover's FBI. What the agents couldn't see is what went on inside the Cal-Neva secluded bungalows after the opening night party had ended. Sam Giancana reportedly told his brother that he had been present at a Kennedy brother's slumber party that night at the Cal-Neva Casino. "The men," he said, "had sex with prostitutes -- sometimes two or more at a time -- in bathtubs, hallways, closets, on floors, almost everywhere but the bed."
In 1961 a Chicago hood named Joseph "Crackers" Mendino died of a heart attack. Over the years, he had worked under everyone from Torrio to Giancana in the juke box, pinball and gambling end of the business. Tony Accardo was one of his pallbearers, and anybody who was anyone in the Chicago outfit was there for the burial, probably the last big-time mob funeral since the days of Al Capone. At the funeral, Accardo and Sam Giancana held a meeting and directed Johnny Roselli to plant in Nevada somebody to watch over Frank Sinatra because the boys had decided that Sinatra was much too enamored with the Kennedy's and wasn't thinking straight anymore. When Roselli returned to the West Coast he called a hood named Lewis McWille, whom he had first met back in 1938, when Roselli did a short stint as the Chicago representative to the Sans Souci Casino in Havana.

McWillie had worked in Cuba for years, mostly for New York racketeer Meyer Lansky. McWillie was never clear to anyone on exactly what it was he did for Lansky, telling the Warren Commission only that he was a "key man" at Lansky's Tropicana Casino in Cuba. When Castro booted Lansky out of Cuba, he brought McWillie with him and placed him inside of his Las Vegas Casino, the Tropicana in Las Vegas. Otherwise, there was very little known about McWillie, who was also used the obvious alias of Lewis N. Martin. It is known that he had deep contacts within the New York and Chicago mobs, and although never a member of any one specific outfit, the FBI kept him under surveillance and considered him to be a top mob hitman and enforcer for hire.

Roselli told McWillie that Chicago wanted him out at Sinatra's Cal-Neva lodge to keep an eye on their investment in the place, and to watch over Sinatra and report his activities back to Roselli. McWillie did as he was told, and created a job for himself at Sinatra's casino, working under the title of "pit boss," but McWillie, a trained card sharp, was no mere pit boss as he made himself out to be. Instead, he was a very rich, seasoned, major gambler who traveled in the highest circles of organized crime, always driven around in a sleek, new limousine and seldom went anywhere without a bodyguard. Whenever he worked in a mobbed up casino, it was always as a high level executive, several times removed from a lowly blackjack dealer on the floor that he purported to be.

At about that same time, McWillie was in frequent contact with Jack Ruby, the man who silenced Lee Harvey Oswald forever. In fact, one of the last persons Ruby spoke to before he leaped on to history's stage was Lewis McWillie. The little that is known about their odd relationship is that, according to what McWillie told the Warren Commission, he and Ruby had known each other from their childhood days in Chicago, and McWillie was Ruby's host for an eight-day vacation in Cuba in August of 1959. That same year, the Dallas Police department's Office of Intelligence listed Jack Ruby and "Chicago-Las Vegas hood Lewis McWillie" as being among those connected with mob run gambling in Dallas.

Gray haired and stylish, McWillie impressed the easily impressible Ruby, who admired McWillie and called him "a very high (class) type person" who reminded Ruby of "Like a banker or a man who understood and enjoyed the finer things in this life, which we are given." Yet, after Ruby gunned down Oswald, the FBI asked him to draw up a list entitled "people who may dislike me" and at the top of the list was Lewis McWillie. On Sunday, November 17, 1963, five days before Kennedy was gunned down, Ruby showed up at the mob owned Stardust Casino in Las Vegas where he invoked McWillie's name to cash a check and was later seen at the equally mobbed up Thunderbird Casino with Lewis McWillie. Two days after meeting McWillie in Las Vegas, Ruby was back in Dallas, flush with enough cash to pay off his back taxes.

The party didn't last long. After only two years, the Cal-Neva was starting to sour on Sinatra and overall only added to the miseries he was having in the summer of 1963. On June 30, 1962, an intoxicated Chuckie English, a Giancana hood, staggered out of the Armory lounge and bumped into one of the FBI agents tagging Giancana. English told the agents that if "Bobby Kennedy wants to know anything about Momo all he had to do was to ask Sinatra."

The agent reported the conversation back to Hoover who brought the comment to Robert Kennedy's attention, who told Hoover to increase the FBI's surveillance on Sinatra and the Cal-Neva. The casino was already being investigated because the Feds suspected that the casino's manager, Skinny D'Amato, was running a statewide prostitution ring out of the place. The agents suspected that the women were being flown in from San Francisco with the operation being run openly from the hotel front desk. Then, a few days after the Chuckie English fiasco, there was the attempted murder of a Cal-Neva employee who was shot on the front steps of the lodge. No one knows if it was mob-related or not, since the incident was hushed up. Then, on June 30, 1962, Deputy Sheriff Richard Anderson came to pick up his beautiful brunette wife at the lodge where she worked as a waitress because she had been one of Sinatra's girlfriends for a while before she married Anderson, three months before. Anderson had noticed the way Sinatra stared at his wife and heard about the rude and off color remarks he made to her and the Deputy, who was twice Sinatra's tiny size, warned the singer to stay away from her. Sinatra backed down and apologized and promised to leave the woman alone. But Sinatra was a man who brooded and let things build up inside him and on the night Anderson came to pick up his wife, as he stopped by the kitchen to talk with some of the help there, Sinatra came in, saw Anderson and ran up to him and screamed at him, "What the fuck are you doing, here?" Anderson remained calm and said he was waiting for his wife, then, suddenly, while the cop was still in mid-sentence, Sinatra grabbed him and tried to throw him out, and after a brief wrestling match, Anderson ended up punching Sinatra so hard in the face that he couldn't perform on stage for a week. Several weeks later, on July 17, 1962, Anderson and his wife were driving down Highway 28, not far from the Cal-Neva, when they were driven off the road by a late model maroon convertible with California plates, driving at high speeds. Anderson lost control of his car, skidded off the road and smashed into a tree, and was killed instantly. His wife was thrown from the car, and suffered severe broken bones and fractures. Anderson's parents said, "We still think to this day that Sinatra had something to do with our son's death." The Andersons left behind four children. But Sinatra's troubles with the Cal-Neva weren't over yet. A few days after Anderson was murdered, and one week before her own death, Marilyn Monroe, flew to the Cal-Neva at Frank

Sinatra's invitation. Sinatra told Monroe that he wanted to discuss their upcoming film together, What a Way to Go. Monroe didn't want to go, but someone told Marilyn that Bobby Kennedy would be there. It sounded logical to Monroe, since it had been in the papers that the Attorney General was in Los Angeles on business.

Sinatra flew Monroe out on his own plane along with Peter Lawford, although the crooner was no longer speaking to Lawford after the Kennedy's dumped him, and Law ford's wife, Patricia Kennedy Lawford. Exactly what happened that weekend, at the Cal-Neva, isn't known and may never be known. Louis McWillie, an outfit related gambler who worked for Sinatra at the Cal-Neva said "There was more to what happened up there than anybody has ever told. It would have been a big fall for Bobby Kennedy."

What is known is that there was dinner with Sam Giancana, Peter and Pat Lawford, Sinatra and Monroe. Giancana, of course, had no business being in the Cal-Neva since he was listed in the state's Black Book of persons forbidden to enter a casino, in fact, he was at the top of the list of restricted persons, but, as San Francisco new columnist Herb Caen said, "I saw Sinatra at the Cal-Neva when Sam Giancana was there. In fact I met Giancana through Frank. He was a typical hood, didn't say much. He wore a hat at the lake, and sat in his little bungalow, receiving people." During the dinner, Monroe got uncontrollably drunk and was led by to the cabin where, while she was passed out, several hookers, male and female, molested her while Sinatra and Giancana watched, with Giancana taking his turn with the actress as well.

While the female prostitutes had their way with Monroe, someone snapped photographs of the entire thing and before the night was over, Sinatra then brought the film to Hollywood photographer Billy Woodfield, and gave him a roll of film to develop in his darkroom.   The next morning, Peter Lawford told Monroe that Robert Kennedy was in Los Angeles and that he didn't want to see her, speak to her or have any contact with her in the future. When she protested, someone showed her the photographs from the night before. That afternoon, she tried to commit suicide with an overdose of pills and had to have her stomach pumped. Later on, when Giancana told the story to Johnny Roselli, Roselli said to Giancana, referring to either Monroe or Campbell, "You sure get your rocks off fucking the same broad as the (Kennedy) brothers, don't you?"

Exactly a year later, Sinatra's involvement with the Cal-Neva came to an end when the McGuire sisters were scheduled to perform there, mostly due to the fact that Giancana was dating Phyllis McGuire, with whom he shared a chalet with during her performance there.   Unfortunately for Giancana, McGuire, Sinatra and the Cal-Neva, the FBI photographed the hood playing golf with Sinatra and having drinks and dinner together in the Cal-Neva dining room. The FBI was also watching that same evening when, during a small party in McGuire's room, Victor LaCroix Collins, the sisters' road manager, became irritated when Phyllis McGuire kept walking by his seat and punching him on the arm. "So I told her," Collins said, "You do that again and I'm going to knock you right on your butt. A half an hour later she punches me again and so I grabbed her by both arms and meant to sit her in the chair I got out of, but I swung around and missed the chair, she hit the floor. She didn't hurt herself . . . but Sam came charging across the room and threw a punch at me wearing a huge big diamond ring that gouged me in the left eye. "I just saw red then and grabbed him, lifted him clean off the floor and I was going to throw him through the plate glass door, but thought, why wreck the place? So, I decided to take him outside and break his back on the hard metal railing on the patio. I got as far as the door and then got hit on the back of the head. I don't know who hit me from behind but the back of my head was split open. It didn't knock me out but I went down with Sam underneath me, he had on a pearl gray silk suit and blood from my eye was running all over his suit. I had a hold of him by the testicles and the collar and he couldn't move; that's when Sinatra came in with his valet George, the colored boy, they were coming to join the party, the girls were screaming and running around like a bunch of chickens in every direction because nobody knew what was going to happen. George just stood there with the whites of his eyes rolling around and around in his black face because he knew who Sam was and nobody ever fought with Sam. . . . Sinatra and George pulled me off of Sam, who ran out the door."

The next morning, the FBI, which had a fairly clear idea of what had happened the night before, as a well as several rolls of film of Sinatra with Giancana, filed its report, with photographs, with the State of Nevada gambling control board. After reading the report, the control board's chairman, Ed Olson, called Sinatra at the Sands Casino in Las Vegas and asked about Giancana being on the property and Sinatra said that he saw a man who looked like Giancana and that they just waved and nodded to each other and that was all. But the FBI also had wind of the fight and told the investigators and flew to Nebraska to interview Collins, who filled them in, and then back to Sinatra who denied knowing anything about it. Olson thanked Sinatra for his time and hung up. There was little else he could do. Sinatra was a casino owner, with substantial investments in the state, and he was also a major celebrity who was singularly responsible for drawing tens of thousands of tourists into Nevada. Then the newspapers got hold of the story and backed Olson into a corner, forcing him to remark that his investigation would not conclude until "certain discrepancies in the information provided by various people at Cal Neva could be resolved." Sinatra read that and called Olson and asked him to come to the Cal-Neva for dinner "to talk about this, your statements."

 Olson said that he felt it was inappropriate to be seen at the Cal-Neva having dinner with Sinatra, since the singer was, technically, under investigation by Olson's office, and even if Sinatra weren't under investigation, Olson said, it would still be unacceptable for the Gaming Commissioner to be seen fraternizing with a casino owner.

 "But Frank kept insisting," Olson said, "and I kept refusing the more I refused the madder he got until he seemed almost hysterical. He used the foulest language I ever heard in my life."

To calm Sinatra down Olson agreed to meet Sinatra in Olson's office but Sinatra didn't show up. An hour later Sinatra called Olson in a rage "You listen to me Ed . . . your acting like a fucking cop, I just want to talk to you off the record."

 Olson, in an attempt to take back the high ground that his position required said: "Who I am speaking to?"

 "This is Frank Sinatra! You fucking Asshole! F-R-A-N-K, Sinatra."

Olson avoided the insults and said that any meeting between them would have to be on record in the presence of witnesses.

Sinatra cut him short and screamed, "Now, you listen Ed! I don't have to take this kind of shit from anybody in the country and I'm not going to take it from you people . . . I'm Frank Sinatra!" Sinatra went on and on, until, at one point, Olson warned Sinatra that if he didn't show up for an interview that Olson would have him subpoenaed. "You just try and find me," the singer threatened, "and if you do, you can look for a big fat surprise . . . a big fat fucking surprise. You remember that, now listen to me Ed, don't fuck with me. Don't fuck with me, just don't fuck with me!"

"Are you threatening me?" Olson asked.

"No . . . just don't fuck with me and you can tell that to your fucking board of directors and that fucking commission too."

The next day two investigators came to watch the count at the Cal-Neva and Sinatra yelled across the casino to Skinny D'Amato, "Throw the dirty sons of bitches out of the house." But since the count had already started, the agents left before an incident could be started but came back the next day, only to have D'Amato offer them $100 each "to cooperate." The agents reported the bribe to Olson, who took moves to revoke Sinatra's license.

When the news was announced that Sinatra was under investigation and would probably lose his casino license, very few people in Nevada rushed to his aid. There were a lot of people in Nevada who resented Sinatra, others despised him and very few people felt that he should have gotten a state gaming license in the first place, and the word around the capitol building in Reno was that Sinatra needed to be taught a lesson. The lesson they taught him was to take away his license to operate a casino or hotel in Nevada, thus forcing him to sell not only his 50% in the Cal-Neva, but also his 9% interest in the Sands, about 3.5 million dollars' worth of holdings in 1963.   "I talked to Sam (Giancana) the next day," said Joe Shimon, a Washington, D.C. Police officer assigned to the Central Intelligence Agency, "and he told me that Sinatra had cost him over $465,000 on Cal-Neva. He said, "That bastard and his big mouth. All he had to do was to keep quiet let, the attorneys handle it, apologize and get a thirty to sixty day suspension . . . but no, Frank has to get on the phone with that damn big mouth of his and now we've lost the whole damn place. He never forgave him. He washed Frank right out of his books."
 Nevada's Governor, Grant Sawyer, stood behind the Gambling control board's decision to yank Sinatra's license. However, while the case was still pending, President Kennedy came to the state and was given a caravan parade through the streets of Las Vegas, and found himself sitting in the same car with Governor Sawyer. Kennedy turned to Sawyer, and said, "Aren't you people being a little hard on Frank out here?" The Governor didn't reply, but later repeated what Kennedy had said to Ed Olson, who was startled by the remark. "That's about the highest degree of political pressure you could ever put into the thing," Olson said. But the Cal-Neva incident was, for the Kennedy's, as Peter Lawford said, "The end of old Frankie boy as far as the family was concerned."

Dumping Sinatra from the White House list of favored persons was long overdue. For years, scores of Kennedy's advisors had been after the President to end his highly public relationship with Sinatra. Not that Sinatra was ever really a White House insider to begin with. Just how far out of the Washington loop Sinatra really was, was underscored by Peter Lawford when he said that "During one of our private dinners, the President brought up Sinatra and said, "I really should do something for Frank." Jack was always so grateful to him for all the work he'd done in the campaign raising money. "Maybe," Jack used to say, "I'll ask him to the White house for dinner or lunch. There's only one problem. Jackie hates him and won't have him in the house, so I really don't know what to do."

Sinatra was eventually invited for lunch, but only when Jackie Kennedy was out of the White House and even then, Sinatra was asked to use a side door to the White House, since Kennedy didn't want the press seeing the crooner on the grounds of the Executive Mansion. In fact, according to Lawford, Sinatra was only allowed into the White House twice during the three years of the Kennedy administration, and then only for brief visits. "I don't think he wanted," said Lawford, "reporters to see Frank Sinatra going into the White House, that's why Frank never flew on Air Force One, and was never invited to any of the Kennedy state dinners or taken to Camp David for any of the parties there."

Kennedy, or "Our Mister Prez" as Sinatra called the new Chief Executive, did call Sinatra on an irregular basis, but this was mostly to cover the President's favorite topic, Hollywood gossip.   "When Kennedy would call," said Ole Blue Eyes' English Secretary, "he would smile at everybody, pick up the phone and say "Hi ya Prez." After each one of those calls, Frank pranced around so proud of the fact that the President was ringing him up." But Sinatra was an astute man and sensed he wasn't wanted around the White House and asked why he was being pushed to the side, only to be told by the President's staff that the Kennedy brothers' wives said that they were attending too many "Sinatra summit meetings" and their wives were not happy about it.   Also, aside from being widely disliked by the White House staff, the Kennedy's had been cooling off to Sinatra for some time before they gave him the axe, in part due to the singers often erratic public, and private, life.

The first signs of trouble came back during the election, when Sinatra hired blacklisted writer Albert Maltz to write the screenplay for a film called "The Execution of Private Slovik" from the book by William Bradford Huie, the story was about the only American serviceman executed by the army for desertion since the civil war. Sinatra planned to direct and produce the film himself.   The media, the public and virtually every civic group in the country attacked Sinatra for hiring Maltz, but the ever feisty Sinatra refused to back down, in large part because he was doing the right thing, and in some part, because he was, simply, a man who wouldn't be told how to live his personal life. Boston's Cardinal Cushing, a close friend of the family, told Joe Kennedy that his son could be hurt in the conservative Catholic vote by Sinatra's hiring a communist and Governor Wesley Powell of New Hampshire had already accused Kennedy of being soft on communists. The Ambassador called Sinatra and said, "It's either us or Maltz, make up your mind, Frank." Sinatra fired Maltz, but it didn't matter. The American Legion got hold of it and went on the attack. The New York Times wrote a long piece about it and John Wayne, then the country's leading box office producer, attacked Sinatra and Kennedy for being soft on Reds.   "God what a mess!" Lawford said. "The Ambassador took care of it in the end, but it was almost the end of old Frankie boy as far as the family was concerned." Sinatra had tempted his fate with highly publicity sensitive Kennedy's, once too often. Especially after word leaked out to the press that he was partners with the mob in a New England racetrack.   Like everyone else on the inside, the Kennedy's knew about Sinatra's overwhelming desire to be around the rough-edged set. Even while Sinatra was helping JFK into the White House he maintained his ownership in the Villa Capri, LA's most mobbed up restaurant that was a home away from home for every displaced Wise guy who traveled west to make a name for himself. But, owning a piece of a restaurant where small-time hoods ate was a different thing from buying into a major Rhode Island racetrack with crime bosses Raymond Patriarca, Tommy Lucchese, and New Jersey's gangster Angelo "Gyp" De Carlo.

When word of the racetrack investment reached the White House, combined with Frankie's mysterious role in introducing Judy Campbell to the President, it was decided to drop Sinatra once and for all. The catalyst behind giving Sinatra the axe, was, of course, Robert Kennedy. As far as the Attorney General was concerned, Sinatra's loyalties really lay with the mob, and, when and if, a push came to a shove, Kennedy was sure, true or not, that Sinatra would go along with the mob in blackmailing the President to get what it wanted.

Dropping Sinatra wasn't a tremendous loss for the White House, they had gotten what they wanted out of Frank, and, if they ever needed him again, they knew that all they would have to do would be to snap their fingers and he'd come running.   To neutralize Sinatra, and always aware of their place on the historical record, the Kennedy's justified dropping Sinatra, by having one of Robert Kennedy's employees at the Justice department suddenly "discover" that Sinatra had ties to organized crime, by reading a Department of Justice report about extortion in the movie business which mentioned Sinatra. To be absolutely certain that Sinatra, and everyone else, understood that he had been axed, the Kennedy boys decided to humiliate him publicly.   Towards the end of January 1962, Peter Lawford, at John Kennedy's request, asked Sinatra if Kennedy could stay at his Palm Springs home in March while Kennedy was out west for a fund raiser. Sinatra was honored and rushed into a massive renovations program on his estate, including building separate cottages for the secret service and installing communications with twenty-five extra phone lines and a huge helipad with a pole for the President's flag.

When everything was set, and Sinatra had bragged and boasted to all of Hollywood that he would host the President, the President called Peter Lawford into the Oval office and said: "I can't stay at Frank's place while Bobby's handling the investigation of Giancana. See if you can't find me someplace else. You can handle it Peter. We'll handle the Frank situation when we get to it." Lawford was terrified of the thought of calling Sinatra with the bad news, and when he did, Lawford, who probably didn't know why the President had changed his plans, blamed the secret service and security reasons for the change in Kennedy's plans. "Frank was livid," Lawford said. "He called Bobby every name in the book and then he rang me up and reamed me out again. He was quite unreasonable, irrational really. [His valet] George Jacobs told me later that when he got off the phone he went outside with a sledgehammer and started chopping up the concrete landing pad of his heliport. He was in frenzy."

Things went from bad to worse when Sinatra learned that Kennedy was staying at the home of Republican Crooner, Bing Crosby. Sinatra, according to Lawford, "telephoned Bobby Kennedy and called him every name and a few that weren't in the book. He told RFK what a hypocrite, that the mafia had helped Jack get elected but weren't allowed to sit with him in the front of the bus." A few months afterwards the truth hit the Mafia as well. All bets were off, the Kennedy's had not only double-crossed the outfit, they had secretly declared war against it. As far as allowing Joe Adonis back into the country, as was agreed before the West Virginia primary, the mob was informed by Joe Kennedy, through Skinny D'Amato, that the Kennedy's not only intended to renege on the deal, they were going to start deporting and locking up hoods on a nationwide basis. The national crime commission called Giancana on the carpet for an answer and in turn Giancana called Sinatra on the carpet right after he got back from the commission meeting. One of his underlings heard Giancana screaming into a phone, "Eat'n out of my hand! That's what Frank told me! Jack's eat'n out of the palm of my hand! Bullshit! That's what that is!" and then watched as the mobster threw the telephone across the room.

Another factor that may have sparked the Kennedy-Sinatra split was Sam Giancana's dabbling in the Caribbean. In the spring of 1961, Frank Sinatra, Sam Giancana tumbled into the life of Porfirio. Rubirosa's life when Rubirosa, Sinatra, Peter Lawford and Dean Martin rented a luxury yacht in Germany and met with Rubirosa and his wife Odile off the French coast. Sinatra may have acted as the conduit between the mob, Rubirosa and the elite within the Dominican Republic which was plotting to overthrow the island insane dictator Raphael Trujillo. With a verbal commitment, by way of Rubirosa, from the Dominican Republic's elite that the mob would be free to operate there once Trujillo was gone, all that Rubirosa had to do was to assure the Kennedy's that if it assisted in the Dominican military in replacing Trujillo in a coup, that the new government would be pro-United States.

In 1961, one of the many things that the Chicago mob wanted was a replacement for Cuba, so they looked around for a small, poor country, close to the United States, one that could be easily controlled, preferably run by a corrupt dictator who would allow the outfit to build its casinos on his sandy shores and stockpile its dirty money in phony banks created just for them. Central America had potential. The Outfit and their occasional partners, the CIA, virtually ran the place anyway, but it was hot, and undeveloped and poor, real poor. And if there was one thing gambling tourists in search of a good time didn't want, it was to look at sweaty, poor, undeveloped locals. Then the boys stumbled on the Dominican Republic, just off the Florida coast. It fit the bill exactly. The problem was that, the island's dictator, Raphael Trujillo, was not only losing his mind, he showed signs of warming up to the Soviet bloc. If that happened, the US would pull its support from the island, and the outfit would have to find another country to corrupt.

Trujillo had his own contacts within the mob. For decades, he and Joe Bonanno, out of New York, had been in various businesses together. When the Kennedy administration broke relations with the Republic, Trujillo traded dope for stolen guns. Still, the Republic had real potential for Chicago, who weren't greatly concerned for Joe Bonanno, a man they held in contempt. All the mob needed to do was get the Kennedy administration to commit to its continuing support to the Republic with or without Trujillo in charge. And that's when the boys discovered the legendary Dominican Playboy, Porfirio Rubirosa, El Rubirosa.

Rubirosa had spent most of his life in Palm Beach and New York bars trying, and succeeding most of the time, in seducing rich socialites, but he was also a roving ambassador for the Dominican Republic, with two primary duties. One was to make sure companies doing business with his father-in-law's government understood that they were to pad their bills with an extra 15%, which would be kicked back to the dictator's New York based holding companies. His other duty was to keep track of American based dissidents to Trujillo's reign. Using well paid mob contacts, Rubirosa turned information on the dissidents over to Trujillo's feared and brutal secret police, the SIM, which was under the control of Colonel John Abbes Garcia. He ran the secret police, the SIM (Servicio Intelligencia Militar), which dogged Dominicans all over the world. On more than one occasion, the SIM simply turned their murderous chores over to one of New York Mafia families to complete. The SIM and the mob kidnapped Dr. Jesus E. Galindez, a lecturer at Columbia University on March 12, 1956. Galindez had been an outspoken opponent of Trujillo. Two versions were advanced. One was that the SIM kidnapped him and threw him into a ship's furnace. The other is that he was returned to the Dominican Republic and Trujillo himself tortured him. The kidnap murder caused a minor international outrage, and to quell the public, Trujillo hired a New York law firm to investigate the disappearance, but all they could come up with was that Galindez had disappeared.

El Rubirosa

Porfirio Rubirosa didn't seem the type to run an international terrorist squad. A Dominican by birth, Rubirosa's father had been a general in the army and later the chargé d'affaires in Paris where Rubirosa grew up in the best schools and amongst the best people. He returned to the Dominican Republic in 1926 to study law at the age of 17 but left school to start a military career. By age twenty, he was a captain and came to the attention of President Trujillo who one day sent the handsome young captain to the airport to pick up his daughter, the plain looking Flor d'Oro -- Rubirosa took the hint and married the girl. Trujillo eventually rewarded the young Rubirosa's good sense by appointing him the position his father had held in Paris and even when Rubirosa divorced Trujillo's daughter in 1940, he managed to stay in the dictator's good graces and was allowed to retain his diplomatic position as well.   After his divorce, Rubirosa married the French film star Danielle Darrieux and then American tobacco heiress Doris Duke, in 1947. When told that he would have to sign a pre-nuptial agreement minutes before the marriage took place, Rubirosa was so infuriated he smoked a cigarette throughout the entire ceremony. Afterwards, in an effort to soothe him over, Duke presented Rubirosa with a check for $500,000.00, several very expensive sports cars and a converted B-25 airplane, since he was also a pilot, and a string of polo ponies. The marriage lasted for thirteen months. Next, in 1953, Rubirosa married Woolworth heiress Barbara Hutton, his fourth wife, while carrying on an affair with the much married Zsa Zsa Gabor. He would later be named in her divorce petition. His marriage to Hutton lasted only 53 days during which time Hutton gave him, or spent on him, no less than $3.5 million in cash and gifts.

Rubirosa was the ultimate pleasure seeker who loved the elegant life. Most nights would be spent dining on exotic foods and then drinking and dancing the rest of the evening away to the Latin rhythms that were then so popular with the international set then. "He also suffered," said a friend, "from a rare disease called priapism which kept him in an almost constant state of sexual arousal and left him unable to be sexually satisfied. He rarely achieved orgasms during sex and then only after hours of struggle. He knew that thing of his was his potential meal ticket and he actually trained to keep it in peak condition. He did exercises for it. He would drink each day a potion called pago-palo which he said came from the bark of a certain tree in the Dominican Republic, he believed that it guaranteed performance ... I once saw him balance a chair with a telephone book on it atop his erection. He said to me, "It's a muscle like any other, it can be strengthened." It's also not known if Sinatra set up the meeting, but after his cruise with Sinatra off the French coast, Rubirosa was invited to meet President Kennedy at his summer house on Cape Cod in late September. Rubirosa would be in the States anyway. The Manhattan District Attorney had summoned him to New York to question him about his role in the mob related kidnap-torture of several Dominican exiles. The day before Rubirosa, Sinatra and the president met in Cape Cod, Sinatra had spent the afternoon at the White House with performers Danny Kay and Judy Garland, teaching the staff how to make Bloody Mary's and then sipping them out on the rear balcony that overlooks the Washington monument. The next day, Sinatra took the president's private plane to the Kennedy's summer home on Cape Cod with Peter and Pat Lawford, Ted Kennedy and Porfirio Rubirosa and his wife Odile. The party went sailing on the president's boat, The Honey Fitz, for three and a half hours, during which Sinatra told everyone about his trip to Italy and his meeting with the Pope. When he was finished, a drunken Peter Lawford said, "All your friends in Chicago are Italian too, huh Frank?"

It will probably never be known what Kennedy, Sinatra and Rubirosa discussed out on the Cape, but less than a month after the meeting, John Kennedy gave CIA Director Alan Dulles the okay to assassinate Trujillo and Sam Giancana began his plans to rebuild the Dominican Republic into another pre-Castro Cuba. Everything was moving along smoothly, until one of Bobby Kennedy's bugs picked up on Giancana's plans to turn the Dominican Republic into another Cuba, with the White House as an unwitting co-conspirator. Kennedy was enraged at Giancana's gall and ordered the FBI to "lockstep" the mob boss. Wherever Giancana went, the FBI was there. The pressure from the lockstep got to Giancana and came to a head when Giancana and Phyllis McGuire were returning from Las Vegas to O'Hare airport. When Sam emerged from the plane, with McGuire's hat and pocketbook in hand, FBI agent Roemer "whistled and howled at the gangster and told him how pretty he looked." "That bastard," Giancana said, "started whistling and saying I was queer and everything like that. I wanted to kill him. People gathered around, we were screaming back and forth. Man oh man, it was fuckin' ridiculous....He wanted me to throw a punch, that's what he wanted, the lousy cocksucker."

As Giancana and McGuire raced down the airport's hallways, the agents walking only inches away from Giancana and McGuire kept "telling me what a great ass I had," as Sam said later. Finally Giancana turned and said "Why don't you fellows leave me alone, I'm one of you?" referring to the CIA plot to kill Castro.
"Oh really?" said FBI agent Roemer, "Come on Momo, show us badge."
When Giancana walked away in disgust, Roemer said "Oh come on Moe, we'll show you ours if you show us yours."
Giancana flung himself around to face the agents and screamed, "What do you want to know? Ask me. Go ahead. Anything you want to know. Go ahead."
"OK, tell us what you do for a living."
"That's an easy one. I own Chicago. I own Miami. I own Las Vegas."
More words were exchanged and finally agent Roemer lost control and yelled out to the crowd that had surrounded them.

"Sam Giancana, this slime, is the boss of the underworld here in Chicago, this slime. You people are lucky you're just passing through Chicago and you don't have to live with this jerk."

Momo stuck his face into Roemer's and said: "Roemer you light a fire here tonight that will never go out we'll get you if it's the last thing we do!"

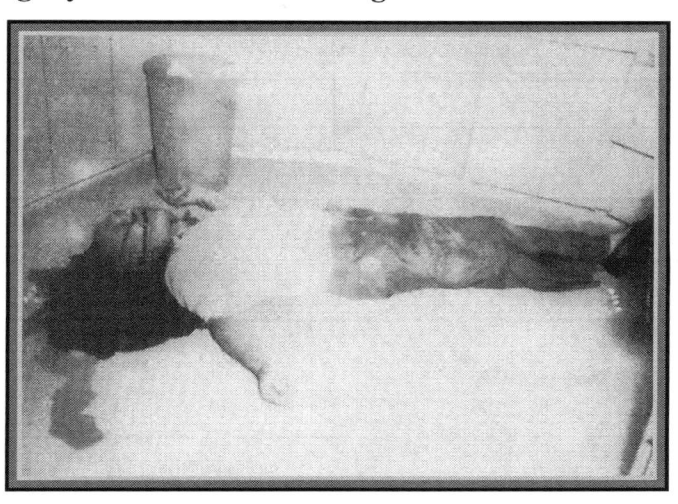

Giancana dead

The day after the airport incident, Giancana was still fuming and talking about killing FBI agent Roemer. Cooler heads prevailed and Giancana called off the contract on the agent's life. Tony Accardo, Giancana's boss, called off the contract, the next day. As for Rubirosa, in 1968 he ran his sports car, at an estimated 97 miles per hour, into a tree along the French coast and was killed instantly.

*****

Goodman Oscar Baylin: Mob lawyer. Born July 26, 1939. Law office Goodman, Chesnoff and Keach at 520 South Fourth Street, Las Vegas. The son of a Philadelphia prosecutor. Goodman graduated from the University of Pennsylvania Law School in 1964 and shortly afterwards went to work as Chief Deputy Public Defender in Clark County, Nevada from 1966 to 1967.

Goodman entered private practice in 1968 and soon represented Mafia and organized crime figures like Meyer Lansky, Anthony Spilotro, Frank Rosenthal, Jimmy Chagra, Phil Leonetti, Nick Civella, Natale Richichi, Nicky Scarfo, Vinny Ferrara and others. Yet, Goodman claimed he had no idea that the Chicago and Kansas City mob ran four casinos in Las Vegas (The Stardust, Fremont, Marina, and Hacienda)

Goodman customer Nicky Scarfo

On June 8, 1999, Goodman was elected Mayor of Las Vegas and reelected in 2003 and in 2007. That same year he was voted Least Effective Public Official in the *Review-Journal*'s annual reader's poll. Not surprisingly, Goodman supported legalized prostitution as a mean of revitalizing Las Vegas.

He also once touted the benefits of drinking gin to a fourth grade class. In 2002, Goodman was a spokesman for Bombay Sapphire Gin. He claimed to have donated his $100,000 fee to local charity, which included half of the money going to his wife's private school, the Meadows. He was charged with trying to use his office to forward his son Ross's career but a formal reprimand was never given. In 2005, he further added to the city's slimy reputation by during a pictorial shoot with topless models.

*****

Greenbaum Murder case: After the Outfit killed Bugsy Siegel, the Flamingo's next manager was Gus Greenbaum, who started in the rackets with Al Capone and who handled the wire service out West for the Chicago outfit. Greenbaum was a master of the skim, the money stolen from the casino winnings before it could be taxed, and unlike Siegel, Greenbaum was a professional, he was a man who could be trusted and depended upon. Greenbaum did his job. The hotel was completed and enlarged from 97 to two hundred rooms. By the end of the year the casino posted a $4 million dollar profit, $15 million before the skim, clearing the way for the skimming to begin. With that kind of cash flooding into the mob's offshore accounts, all of the mob families moved in to grab a piece of Las Vegas, but it was the Chicago outfit that built Vegas and they did it with the cash, tens upon tens of millions of dollars, they took from the Teamsters Central Pension Funds.

Greenbaum

The outfit had sent Greenbaum west to Phoenix, Arizona in 1928 to manage the Southwest division of its wire service, Trans-American. In the early forties, he was moved to Vegas where he took over the Flamingo after the Bugsy Siegel murder, and put the place in the black within the first six months of his management. By 1950, Greenbaum was widely recognized as the driving force behind the success of the $50 million Tropicana as well as being known and respected in the underworld as a reliable source of information on Las Vegas real estate. Like Willie Bioff, Greenbaum lived in Arizona, part time, and was close to Barry Goldwater, then a Phoenix Arizona Councilman. In fact, Goldwater's family operated a branch of Goldwater's Department store inside the Desert Inn, which was the excuse Goldwater used for visiting Vegas so often.

After his phenomenal success at the Flamingo and the Tropicana, Greenbaum was called in to put the Riviera Casino in the black after the place lost five million dollars for its original investors. Greenbaum didn't want the job, but Tony Accardo and Jake Guzak, the Chicago mob's money manager and technically, Greenbaum's boss, personally flew out to Phoenix to try to persuade him to take the position at the Riviera. Greenbaum heard them out, but turned the job down, because, he told them the strain of correcting the outfit's stupid mistakes was starting to take its effects on him. After seven years on the hot seat, he had enough. He was tired, he was rich and he wanted to retire away from Vegas to Phoenix. Accardo and Guzak said they understood and returned to Chicago.

A week later, Greenbaum's sister-in-law was found murdered in her bedroom. The message was received. Greenbaum moved back to Vegas to run the Riviera for a 27% interest in the place. This time he lasted only three years. In 1958 Johnny Roselli, who was close to Greenbaum, was told by Paul Ricca and Accardo to order Greenbaum to step down. He was addicted to heroin, drunk when he wasn't high, running around with women half his age who stole from him, and was deeply in debt from gambling at the tables, losing up to $20,000 a week. Worst of all, he was skimming from the joint, "Beyond," said Johnny Roselli, "what Mooney (Giancana) and the guys back in Chicago considered reasonable." Roselli went out to Vegas and gave Greenbaum the order, he was to sell his share in the Riviera to one of the outfit's front men and leave town. Do that, he could live. All past transgressions forgiven. But Greenbaum refused. "This town is in my blood, Johnny," he told Roselli and went right back to stealing from the skim.

On December 3, 1958, the police found Greenbaum dead in bed, his throat was cut so completely, that his head was almost falling off. Down the hall, in a different bedroom, they found Greenbaum's wife's throat cut as well. She had been knocked out with a heavy bottle, which caved in the right side of her eye. Newspapers were piled around her to keep the blood from staining the carpet. The Chicago outfit, which, by mob standards anyway, normally showed a loyalty to those who served it, would have let Greenbaum's sins go. After all, he had made them a fortune, but Meyer Lansky had a piece of the Riviera and pushed for Greenbaum's demise. "That was Meyer's (Lansky's) contract," gangster Johnny Roselli said years later.

*****

Hearse: While doing in business in Las Vegas, the high profile Giancana sometimes conducted his business in a rented hearse to throw off federal agents assigned to follow him.

*****

Johnson, Lyndon: For decades, Washington, DC insiders had wondered aloud about how Lyndon Johnson, a professional public servant all of his life, had acquired a fortune which included a radio and television station, considerable real estate and bank holdings worth a total of $15,000,000.

Johnson caused the whispers himself. He made no attempts to hide his wealth, instead, in true LBJ fashion, he flaunted it. He owned a 414-acre ranch in Texas, which included a 6,300ft landing strip and two planes and an enormous and very expensive estate, the Elms, in exclusive Northwest Washington.

Life was good for the former high school janitor who worked his way through college. For almost ten years he had been one of the most powerful men on the Hill, and as Vice President, his career still had promise.

Then, in March of 1962, the FBI arrested Billie Sol Estes, a big time contributor to the Democratic party from West Texas, on charges of fraud and theft for his role in a multimillion-dollar deal involving storage tanks, fake montages and cotton allotments which would eventually lead to the dismissal of several Agricultural Department officials.

Estes

Slowly, word leaked out to the public, for most of inside Washington already knew the allegations, that LBJ and Estes had been business partners in several ventures and that Johnson had lobbied on Estes' behalf at the Agriculture Department, that Johnson had tried to block the FBI's investigation and that he had received many gifts from Estes' office including an airplane.

There's some evidence to suggest that Johnson worked a deal with Hoover to suppress the evidence against him in the Estes case or that after Kennedy was killed, that Johnson simply ordered Hoover to destroy the evidence against him.

The Kennedy's were worried over the Estes business, especially when they learned that a Republican congressman was planning to use the Estes business to impeach Johnson.

Relations between the Johnson and Kennedy families had always been tense. During the democratic presidential primary in 1960, when Johnson was in the race for the White House, his staff spread stories that the Kennedy brothers were "cross-dressing homosexuals" and that certain Staff members had photographs from a party in Las Vegas to prove it.

Somebody also broke into the Kennedy doctors' office and ransacked the place and a few days later, Texan John Connelly, a Johnson supporter held a press conference to announce that Kennedy had Addison's disease and would not live long enough to fulfill his term.

Another loser from that primary was Chicago's own Democratic king maker, Jacob Arvy, who backed LBJ against Kennedy and as a result had no influence with the Kennedy White House.

In the middle of the Estes mess, Henry Marshall, an Agriculture Department official in Texas who was investigating the Estes case, ended up dead. Although Marshall's face, hands and arms were bruised and he had been shot five times with a bolt-action rifle, meaning that each shot required a pump to eject the shell, the death was ruled a suicide.

Estes would later claim that Marshall was killed by a convicted killer named Mac Wallace and that the murder was contracted by LBJ.

Just as the Estes mess was erupting, the Bobby Baker scandal exploded.

Bobby Baker of Pickens, South Carolina, started his career in Washington as a Senate Page in 1942. Twenty-one years later, at age 34, he was personnel secretary to the Majority leader and was a major power on Capitol Hill and was known, rightfully, as the 101st Senator of the United States.

Starting in the 1950s, Baker became Johnson's protégée or "Little Lyndon" as he was sarcastically called.

LBJ's aide Harry McPherson recalled Baker by saying "He was very smart, very quick, and indefatigable. Just worked all the time. He was always running someplace to make some kind of a deal."

By 1960, Bobby Baker was the man to see on Capitol Hill. He not only knew where the bodies were buried, he probably buried them there. He was also a millionaire, an odd circumstance for a man who was born into humble surroundings and never worked outside government.

There were always rumors about Baker's involvement with the mob but the connections were never made clear until 1962.

For years, the Trujillo dictatorship that ran the Dominican Republic had been trying to influence Bobby Baker to their side.

All the attempts failed until Baker learned that Intercontinental Hotels Corporation, which was then wholly owned by Pan American Airlines, was considering expanding his casinos into the Caribbean, specifically into the business friendly Dominican Republic.

Intercontinental already had 23 hotels in the Caribbean, three of which housed casinos which had been set up to lure tourist into the hotel, tourist who would use Pan Am Airways to get there.

But the company didn't want to run the casinos because they considered it unseemly and instead set out to find a company which would run the casinos for them.

At that point, somebody brought in Bobby Baker, largely because Pan Am Airway, InterContinental's owner, was subject to strict federal airline regulations and it was well known that Pan Am wanted those regulations relaxed and Baker had enough power on Capitol Hill and the White House to make that happen.

Baker called InterContinental's chairman and arranged an appointment to see him, but on the day of the appointment, Baker showed up with mobster Ed Levison, brother to the infamous Louis "Sleep-Out Louie" Levison, who was the original manager of Myer Lansky's casino, the Havana Riviera in Cuba, and was now running the Fremont in Las Vegas which was secretly owned by Tony Accardo, Sam Giancana and Paul Ricca.

It was also at Accardo's request that Levison managed to get then Senator Lyndon Johnson and Baker as his first official guests at the opening of the Stardust casino back in 1955.

Baker and the Levison brothers had been involved in a series of questionable business deals over the years; in fact Sleep-Out Levison consigned a $175,000 business loan for Baker a few months before the meeting.

Now Baker wanted Intercontinental to allow Levison to run their casinos for them in Santo Domingo, the Dominican Republic.

Intercontinental executives explained to Baker that other bids were already under consideration and that one of the bids had been submitted by Cliff Jones, the former Lieutenant Governor of Nevada.

But, unknown to Intercontinental, Jones was already partners with the Levison brothers in a shady Caribbean bank as well as several Las Vegas Casinos.

Baker said, "I'll talk to Cliff, we're very close" and added that he and Jones and Kozloff could operate the casino together and, in theory, Intercontinental agreed.

At the next meeting, Intercontinental told Baker and Levison that the deal would fall apart if his brother, Sleep-Out Louie, were involved in the casino because of his criminal record and contacts to the underworld.

Levison assured the corporation that his brother would have nothing to do with the casinos despite the fact that Ed Levison himself also ran a mob-connected gambling empire and had five felony arrests on his record.

It was finally decided that they would merge the Jones bid with Bobby Baker and Levison bid for control of the casinos, however, when the final bid was submitted, it only showed Jones' name on it.

Baker, Levison and Jones won the bid of course and were given control over the hotel-casinos, not only in the Dominican Republic but in Curacao, British Antilles and Quito Ecuador as well.

With control of the casino in the Dominican Republic, all Baker and Levison had to do now was to get assurances from the island's iron-fisted ruler, Trujillo, that they would be allowed to operate safely and undisturbed.

Trujillo, who was as corrupt as a leader could be, agreed. However, shortly before the Baker-Levison plan could fall into place, Trujillo was murdered by his own military guards on orders from the CIA.

In December of 1962, with Trujillo out of the way, the Dominican Republic held its first free election and a victory for Juan Bosch of the Partido Revolucionario Dominicano ensued.

Bosch, who had been exiled by Trujillo for twenty-five years, was a progressive in the democratic tradition and Kennedy instructed the state department to give Bosch its full support. With communism making rapid advancements throughout Latin America and the Caribbean, Kennedy hoped to make the Dominican Republic under Bosch a democratic showplace.

Vice President Johnson, Bobby Baker and Ed Levison were in the Dominican Republic as guests of the Bosch government to witness Bosch's swearing in. Afterwards, Baker flew to Miami Beach where he met with Sam Giancana and Sigelbaum at the International hotel in Miami Beach.

It was probably at this meeting that Baker convinced Giancana that the Dominican Republic, which on the surface anyway, looked stable enough, could be the mob's replacement for Cuba.

A few weeks later, the FBI learned that Giancana did, in fact, intend to open casinos in the Dominican Republic.

Perhaps at that point it all came together for Bobby Kennedy, who may have recognized all the signs of pending scandal and decided to close it down before it exploded.

Kennedy ordered the FBI to place a lockstep on Giancana. No matter where he went or what he did, six to ten FBI agents dogged his every move. Agents would even stand next to Giancana at public urinals and insult the size of his manhood.

Agents followed his daughters, his caretakers and his girlfriends. They knocked on neighbors' doors and asked if they knew that a notorious gangster was living on the block.

The pressure of surveillance put on by the FBI forced Giancana to shut down extortion rackets and gambling operations.

"You tell everyone," Giancana said at a meeting with his Capos, "that everything is off. This is because of the G. We ain't spending another nickel. Everyone is on their own. They got to make it any way they can."

The same pressure was being applied out in Las Vegas as well and the skim was slowed down which dried up the cash flow in to mob coffers from Boston to Los Angles.

Still, when the pressure let up a little bit, Giancana and several other Chicago hoods took a jaunt down to the Dominican Republic to scout out more potential casino sights.

Everything in the Dominican Republic looked good until the Dominican military, backed by the island's land owning class, disposed Juan Bosch and a civilian Junta took over, tossing the Republic into two years of political and social chaos and the mob's hopes of building another Cuba off the American coast were lost forever.

The end of the game for Bobby Baker came shortly afterwards.

In December of 1961, at a pre-inaugural party, Bobby Baker and Vice President Johnson had met with Levison and mobster Benny Sigelbaum and Johnson's neighbor, lobbyist Fred Black and formed the Serve-U-Corporation, which would provide vending machines for companies working on federally granted programs.

The machines were manufactured by a Chicago-based corporation secretly owned by Tony Accardo, Paul Ricca, Gus Alex and Sam Giancana and others.

Baker's connection to the Serve-U-Corporation is what caused his life to come tumbling down in October of 1963 when he was forced to resign his senate post after a vending machine contractor named Baker in a civil suit as the person who strong-armed them out of defense contractors' plant when they refused to kick back enough money.

It turned out that if Baker went down he could have brought John Kennedy and his entire administration with him because Baker was instrumental in introducing John Kennedy to a suspected Russian spy named Ellen Rometsch.

Ellen Rometsch

Rometsch was a stunning young brunette who had found her way out of an East German slum and moved to Washington in 1961 as the wife of a West German Army sergeant assigned to Embassy duty.

Mrs. Rometsch soon became a popular regular at Bobby Baker's Quorum Club up on Capitol Hill, a semi private watering hole for the Capital's elite and earned a well-deserved reputation as a party girl with a very open mind.

Then, sometime around 1962, Bill Thompson, a lobbyist, took Rometsch to meet John Kennedy. According to Thompson, after the meeting, "Jack sent back word. It turned out to be the best time he ever had in his life. That was not the only occasion they met. She saw him again. It went on for a while."

Rometsch started talking about the affair and the FBI, which already suspected that Rometsch was an East German spy, heard about the affair and began to watch Rometsch around the clock.

When the Bobby Baker scandal erupted, J. Edgar Hoover told Bobby Kennedy about Rometsch and her ties to not only Baker but the Soviets and within hours, Rometsch and her husband were deported back to Europe.

By 1963, the Kennedy's were fed up with LBJ, and there was serious talk of dumping him from the ticket the following year "For health reasons."

It never happened.

What did happen, was that one day in Chicago, in April 1963, Jimmy Hoffa was playing cards in his hotel room with Joey Glimco and their lawyers, when Hoffa asked what would happen if something were to happen to Bobby, or "Boo-bee" as he called him, Kennedy. The group responded that John Kennedy would "be so pissed off he would probably replace him with somebody who is a bigger son of bitch then Bobby is."
After a short silence, Hoffa asked, "But what would happen if something happened to John Kennedy?" and the answer was, "Lyndon Johnson would become President and replace 'Boo-bee' as his first act."

In 1965, the FBI had placed a bug on Bobby Baker and those bugs were picking up things that LBJ figured the American people didn't need to know, so, on July 11, 1965, President Lyndon Johnson ordered all of the illegal wiretaps planted by the FBI, including every bug planted against the mob, to be shut down.

*****

Kleinman and Rothkopf: Moe Kleinman and Louis Rothkopf had been members of the old Mayfield Road Mob in Cleveland with Moe Dalitz and Sam Tucker. In the late 1940s, Dalitz, Kleinman, Rothkopf, Tucker and Thomas Jefferson McGinty operated the most powerful gambling syndicates in the Nation. When Dalitz opened the Desert Inn Casino in Las Vegas in 1950, Tucker, Kleinman and Rothkopf were with him. On paper, Dalitz was the treasurer and secretary of the Desert Inn, Kleinman, the onetime prizefighter (12701 Shaker Boulevard, Suite 802, Cleveland) was vice president and Sam Tucker (1347 Biscaya Drive, Surf Side, Miami Beach, Fla.) was on the board of directors and McGinty was the casinos major stockholder. Each of the men owned at least 10 to 12% of the Desert Inn's stock. The actual owners of the casino were Lucky Luciano, Meyer Lansky, Longy Zwillman and a slew of lesser partners including the New England Mafia. Rothkopf and "Pittsburgh" Hymie Martin were suspected of murdering William E. Potter, a Cleveland City councilman on February 3, 1931. In fact, Martin was tried for the murder and was convicted. He won a retrial, however, and was acquitted. By 1951, aside from being vested in the Desert Inn, Kleinman, and Rothkopf owned a series of in and around the Ohio-Kentucky area casinos including the Mound Club, the Pettibone Club, the Jungle Inn, the Beverly Hills Club, and the Lookout House. On Monday evening, March 26, 1951 the televised Kefauver hearings into organized crime grilled New Jersey gangster Abner "Longy" Zwillman and then called Cleveland gangsters Morris Kleinman and Louis Rothkopf to be interviewed. Kleinman and Rothkopf were two of 65 known Cleveland based criminals subpoenaed by the committee, including two other leaders of the old Cleveland Syndicate Moe Dalitz and Sammy Tucker.

Rothkopf was called first. The committee wanted to know about his extensive illegal gambling interests in Ohio, Kentucky, Florida, and Las Vegas. The gangster was in a sour mood and began reading a prepared statement that he undoubtedly wrote himself " I am not an actor and have had no public speaking training. I would be much like an amateur appearing at a disadvantage in front of you who have become like professionals. Newspapers said this was bigger than the World Series. A cartoon in the Cleveland Press suggested that my television debut might replace Kukla, Fran and Ollie. (Children's comical characters) From newspapers, I can demand a retraction or sue for libel. I cannot check on what is happening to me on television or radio. If the television industry wants me to boost their sales, I am entitled to be consulted. This is a violation of my constitutional rights. I will not perform to help TV. I will not proceed further until this apparatus is shut off and removed." There was a very long pause but Senator Kefauver finally asked, "We couldn't find you in Cleveland. If we had you wouldn't have been exposed to this. Do you want the television shut off?"

"I want everything off," Kleinman barked and Kefauver directed that the cameras be turned away from the gangster.

Since the committee had been trying to serve both Kleinman and Rothkopf for over a year, the Senators asked Kleinman where he had been, a reasonable question but he refused to answer. He then refused to acknowledge that he had been convicted of income tax evasion in 1933. (He was released from Lewisburg federal prison in September 1936, after having served 3 years.) He refused to answer any of the next five questions tossed at him. Finally, Kefauver said, "Let the record show that the witness is silent," Senator Charles W. Tobey shouted at Kleinman, "You sat right there behind the other witness for an hour and a half, and you never blinked. Then you come up here and as soon as questions are asked of you, you quail before the lights. It makes me sick to see you try to put up this bluff. Good Lord, no honest man would do that. Before we're through, sir, you'll come to the bar of justice." Louis Rothkopf took the stand next and read a statement which basically repeated what Kleinman's statement said. Rothkopf too refused to answer questions and was arrested. A few days later, both Kleinman and Rothkopf (And ten others) were cited for contempt of Congress for refusing to answer the crime committee's questions. Both convictions were later overturned in court.

*****

Krakower, Esther: Bugsy Siegel's wife. Born 1911 died 1982. Mrs. Benjamin "Bugsy" Siegel and younger sister to Murder Inc. killer Whitey Krakower. A childhood sweetheart of Bugsy Siegel, (Who lived at 158 Princess Street) the married in Brooklyn on January 27, 1929 when she was 17. The couple eventually had two daughters who were already teenagers when their father was murdered. The Siegel's were divorced in Reno, Nevada in December 1946, prior to the opening of the Flamingo Hotel in Las Vegas. Esther returned to New York City to raise their two daughters. She never remarried. She died at age 70 in Bloomfield Hills, Michigan. Her younger brother was Benjamin Krakower AKA Whitey Krakow. (Born 1905. Died July 30, 1941.) Lived at Ageloff Towers, Avenue A and East Fourth Street in Manhattan. Claimed to be an interior decorator. A killer for Murder Incorporated. Whitey Krakower, with Siegel and Frankie Carbo, murdered Harry "Big Greenie" Greenberg in 1939. Several months later Abe Reles and Tick Tock Tannenbaum implicated Krakower in the murder. Siegel assumed that when Krakower was indicted, that he would implicate him in the Greenberg murder and took steps to insure that did not happen. On July 30, 1941, at 7PM, Krakower was sitting on a chair outside a barroom at 49 Willett Street (today it's a city park) when a black sedan with New Jersey plates drove by and fired three shots into Krakower, killing him.

*****

Lansky, Meyer: Mob leader, gambler. Born Meier Suchowljansky. Born August 28, 1900 in Grodno Poland. Parent were Max and Yetta. Died January 15, 1983. Lansky always said that his earliest memories were of ceaseless assaults on the Jewish community he grew up in by the larger gentle world that surrounded them. He recalled often that as a child he could not envision a world that was violently divided between by warfare between Jews and non-Jews. That nightmare ended when the family arrived in New York, by way of Ellis Island, in 1911 when Lansky was eleven years old.

The Lansky family settled in Brooklyn and then to Manhattan's Lower East Side and by all accounts, Lansky was a law abiding teen. At some point, the story varies, Lansky met and befriended Benjamin Bugsy Siege and Lucky Luciano. During Prohibition, Lansky and Lansky, in what was called the Bugs and Meyers Mob, worked as rum running and whisky hijackers, murder for hire, gambling and burglaries. They were eventually absorbed into "Joe the Boss" Masseria Mafia operation, working under Luciano.

By 1931, Lansky was a trusted financial adviser to Luciano and was well respected for his sound judgment by the ruling Commission which he helped to form however, it is not true that he was brains behind organized crime. His one lasting contribution came after the Second World War. In all of his illegal casinos, which stretched from Cuba, Kentucky, New Orleans to Florida, there was no cheating. When a customer won, he was paid and crooked games were forbidden. It was innovative business for the times and it worked. In the next decade, it would work for Las Vegas as well.

Lansky hide most of his income, and taught other, less savvy hoods, how to hide their incomes in numbered bank accounts in Switzerland and later in Bahamian off shore accounts. Contrary to legend, Lansky didn't discover these loop holes. Other mobsters, particularly Tony Accardo and Murray Humphreys in Chicago, had been sheltering cash outside the United States since the early 1930s.

Lansky was an early investor in the Flamingo hotel and was probably one of the prime movers behind the murder of Bugsy Seigel in 1947. He would stay invested in Vegas casinos, such as the Sands, through a series of front men until the very early 1970s.

By 1948, Lansky's Florida paradise was turning sour. Gambling had gotten too far out of hand and the Florida state government, always lax in these issues, began to crack down because the country was changing. Millions of veterans were beginning the great American exodus south and west and Florida was booming. Gambling and gangster, no matter how benign, were bad for the states sparkling image. Lansky sold off his goldmine, the Colonial Inn, but on October 11, 1950, the Kefauver Committee called him in for severe questioning.

Jack Benny at the Flamingo

Lansky lost virtually everything when Fidel Castro shut down the Riviera Hotel in Havana and threw Lansky off of the island in 1960. He was not even able to recoup his loses in building the hotel, estimated to be at around $14 million dollars, an enormous amount of construction money at the time. (Most of the raw materials need to build the luxury hotel had to be imported)
Lansky health, always fragile, got worse after Cuba was lost. He developed ulcers and eventually suffered a heart attack.

In the 1970s, a rumor started that Lansky was worth at least $300 million. The truth was, towards the end of his life Lansky was supposed to have been hard pressed for cash and was having a difficult time making ends meet. His financial problems in large part started because of his inability to go legitimate at the right time. The right time in Lansky's case would have been to follow the example of Moe Dalitz who transformed himself from a common thug to a distinguished and leading citizen in Las Vegas. For whatever reason, Lansky insisted on being a silent and illegal partner in a series of casinos. His legitimate investments, mostly in hotels and golf courses, never seemed to make any money. Desperate, in the 1960s, Lansky became involved in high-risk rackets like drug smuggling, pornography, prostitution and extortion.

Lansky's life was not a happy one. He was born into crushing poverty. His first wife suffered from severe emotional problems. His eldest son was born with cerebral palsy and grew steadily more disabled throughout his life. The federal government hounded Lansky from about 1950 until his death in 1983. During those years, he was either under investigation, under indictment or in court. The FBI, the Justice Department the IRS and the INS built case after case against him. Compounding his problems was that the Mafia could have taken anything they wanted to from him, and there was nothing he could about it.

In the early 1970s, Lansky tried to retire to Israel, moving there under the law of return. However, the federal government wanted Lansky back in the US to face charges of skimming millions of dollars from the Flamingo casino in Las Vegas. Although the

Israeli government refused his request for permanent citizenship in 1971. The story is that when Golda Meir, who had no idea who Lansky was, had the situation explained to her, one of her aides used the word "Mafia". At that, Meir held up her hand and said "Mafia? No Mafia. Israel has enough troubles with the Mafia." Lansky sued but in 1972, the Israeli Supreme Court backed the government decision.

Determined not to return the indictment in the US, Lansky flew to Switzerland, Rio, Buenos Aires, Paraguay, La Paz, Lima and Panama but no country would take. The Paraguayan military government even refused to let him off of the airplane. Finally, he returned to Miami where he was served a subpoena.

Lansky

Finally, in 1973, following heart surgery, Lansky went on trial in Miami and was acquitted largely because the government had no real case against him. But that was not a sticking point with the US Justice Department, which, from one generation after the next, was determined to convict Lansky of something. Lansky's last years were spent quietly at his home in Miami Beach.

Lansky, the man, was an interesting person. Once, while taking his family out to dinner at Embers restaurant in Miami Beach. A man at the table behind them was bragging how well he knew Lansky. The family knew the man had never met Meyer, who had his back to the braggart.

When the meal was over, Lansky stood and walked over to the man's table and shook his hand, asked how he was and why they man didn't come around anymore. It was that sort of gesture that made Lansky a celebrity within the retirement community in Miami.

Always a heavy smoker (Two packs of unfiltered Camel Cigarettes a day) he died of lung cancer on January 15 of 1983.

*****

Magoon, Seymour: was a gunman and killer of note for Murder Inc. (one of the few, if not the only, Irish-American killers in the gang) He vanished in the mid-1940s and has since become a popular legend. Some say Magoon was murdered and buried and his body never found. Another story says that he moved to Nevada, changed his names and lived out his days as a card dealer at the Flamingo Hotel.

*****

Freemont Street, 1920. This would one day be the center of the Vegas Strip

The Outside man: was a living reminder to the Inside men, and the card sharps, con artists and stick up men who considered stealing from casinos, that behind the glitter and glare of the Vegas lights, killers ran the show. It was their casino. It was their money, so smarten up and walk straight. If the boss of a casino had a problem he couldn't handle, he took it to the Outside man. He was the muscle, not the brains in Vegas, and when Chicago called the shot in that town, being their "Representato" was, for wise guys, like being a God.

For almost four decades, the various mob outfits worked well together in Las Vegas. There had been a few nasty incidents, like the one in 1954, when Los Angeles Mafia boss, Jack Dragna, made a sloppy attempt to get a toe hold in Vegas by sending in some sluggers to scare Meyer Lansky's men, Doc Stacher and Moey Sedway.

Moey Sedway

It took the New York families a few days, but they managed to send in several dozen of their best gunmen to match Dragna's invasion force. A shooting war on the strip was avoided, when a peace council was called. The gangs met in Manhattan, and Dragna withdrew his troops after Lansky gave him a cash send off. The New York mobs figured that Chicago's boss, Tony Accardo, was behind the Dragna move, but in the name of peace, they overlooked it. Still, the message was clear. If they didn't want to get muscled out of Gangster Heaven, each of the families would need a strong presence in Vegas. But that didn't work either. By 1958, each organization had sent in its toughest, in some cases, craziest enforcers to represent them on the strip. But, the only thing they accomplished, as Accardo said, "was to scare the fuck'n tourist back to Iowa."

A general syndicate meeting was called, and it was decided that since Chicago had declared itself the arbitrator of all mob business west of the Mississippi, that they would appoint the Outside man, the enforcer, to watch over Vegas, for everyone. It gave Chicago a lot of power, but, on the other hand, having an enforcer in Vegas was overhead. There was no money in it. The real money, the real power, was inside the casinos. And that was another reason for the Outside man to exist. Every outfit had an "Inside man" in Vegas, the low level, business like hood, charged with watching over the "skim," the millions of dollars taken out of the casino's counting rooms before the tally was reported to the government and taxed. Since no one, accept the Inside man, really knew how much the day's count was before it was skimmed, there were persistent rumors that the inside men were stealing from the take. But a little stealing was expected, unavoidable really. However, sometimes the stealing got to be much, and the bosses back home needed to scare the inside men into following the rules. Enter the Outside man. The first hood that Chicago sent to be its God in Vegas was Marshal Caifano, a dangerous man with a hair-trigger temper and the disposition of a rattlesnake. Like Sam Giancana, and most of the hoods who ruled over Chicago in the late 1950s and early 1960s, Caifano came out of the notorious 42 gang that sprung out of Chicago's sprawling Italian Ghettos, and, again like Giancana, Caifano's arrest record dated back to 1929. By 1952 he was already a prime suspect in at least ten mob murders, and, later, won short lived, national recognition when he refused to answer questions before the McClellan committee.

It was Sam Giancana who sent Caifano to Las Vegas in the late 1950s, when the Chicago outfit was skimming a million a day out of its casinos there. Caifano got the job, largely because Giancana decided that he wanted the hood's beautiful wife, Darlene, a tough talking, Kentucky Mountain hillbilly who, according to FBI agent Bill Roemer, modeled herself after Virginia Hill.

Five foot three inch John Marshal Caifano (Left and right)

Sam had a thing for Darlene, and Darlene wanted to taste Giancana's power, so in 1958 the two started to meet regularly on Friday nights in a hotel Giancana owned, the Thunderbird, in suburban Rosemount, outside Chicago. Soon, Sam decided he wanted Darlene on a full-time basis, so, to get Caifano out of the way, the mob boss sent his most trusted solider to Vegas as a replacement for Johnny Roselli, a man Giancana never liked or trusted. It was interesting how Caifano found out about Momo and Darlene too. Special Agent Bill Roemer of the FBI was trailing Giancana and figured out that Giancana and Darlene were having an affair. Roemer decided to use the information to see if he could get Caifano to flip over to the FBI as an informant. Roemer stopped Caifano one night and told him about Giancana and Darlene and then asked "So what do you think about that?" Caifano's face lit up with a smile that went from ear to ear. He couldn't be happier. He thought it was an honor. Roemer, who was relatively new to the job, didn't understand the rules yet, and went away confused, certain that, at the least, a killer like Caifano would fly into a rage. But he didn't. All it did was make him happy, because now Caifano had Sam Giancana just where he wanted him. Sleeping with Caifano's wife was a direct violation of the few rules the Chicago mob has. Caifano could have killed Giancana for what he was doing and got away with it too. But he wouldn't. The affair between his boss and his had gotten him one of the best jobs in organized crime, and Caifano knew that as long as the affair went on, he would hold his position in Vegas.
Tony Accardo, the true boss of the Chicago outfit under Paul Ricca, was appalled with Giancana's selection. Accardo was a man who liked things done quietly, in the shadows, and he knew that Caifano didn't have the suave and sophistication to handle the delicate work needed in Vegas. But Giancana wouldn't budge on his decision. But before Caifano left for Vegas, Accardo called him into Meo's Restaurant, where he conducted most of his business and told him to "lay low in Las Vegas, no one gets hurt without clearing it with us first and don't do nothing to scare the tourists."

And at first, Caifano did as he was told. He laid low and minded his own business. He handled everything safely and quietly. Then he decided to let the city know he was there. He changed his name to John Marshall, dumped the cheap suits and replaced them with expensive, but loud, open neck silk shirts, bedecked himself in gold chains, yellow pants and $500 imported European leather loafers. He asserted Chicago's position and authority by terror and intimidation. Police have long suspected that it was Caifano who placed the bomb under Willie Bioff's truck and slashed Gus Greenbaum's throat. The more people Caifano killed on the bosses' orders, the more belligerent he became, alienating almost everyone in town that had to deal with him.

Caifano never learned that terror worked in the union extortion business, or the protection and loan sharking rackets, but not in Vegas, where cooperation and low profile were the keys to success. There were few people in the Vegas-Mob hierarchy that he didn't manage to threaten, insult or frighten. But, he was Chicago's man, so there was nothing that could be done about it. But, by the start of 1960, the people and the state government started to resent the reputation that the hoodlums in Vegas were giving their state and they decided to do something about it. They drew up legislation that banned known mobsters from their casinos by placing their names, photographs and background information in the so called "Vegas Black Book" and one of its first entrees, behind Sam Giancana, was Marshal Caifano.

Caifano was informed, in writing and in person, to stay out of all of the state's casinos and, if he was seen in the casinos, he would be arrested and casino operators would be fined and eventually lose their license to operate. It was the worst possible thing that could happen to any gangster, much less Chicago's Representative. There were hundreds of mobsters who roamed the streets of Vegas in the early sixties and most of them laid low enough to avoid being included in the book, but Caifano had brought on the problem himself. However, being included in the Vegas Black Book did nothing to slow Caifano down; more than ever before, he stuttered up and down Glitter Gulch making sure the world understood he was Chicago's man in Vegas. In fact, he made a point of not only going into the casinos, he made sure he was spotted.

The Nevada State authorities, who would have been willing to look the other way for the occasional transgression, had no choice but to arrest the mobster in the lobby of the Stardust casino when he entered it three times in one night, after he was warned to stay out. Then, to the horror of Ricca and Accardo, Caifano did the unthinkable. He sued the state of Nevada, taking the state to court to have his name removed from the Black Book. Caifano lost his suit and his name stayed in the exclusion book but the entire episode scared the hell out of Ricca and Accardo. Finally, Paul Ricca stepped in and told Giancana to replace Caifano with Johnny Roselli, whom Caifano had replaced several years before, until they could find someone else to send out to Vegas.

Although Giancana despised Roselli, he had to acknowledge that Caifano wasn't working out, and that Roselli did have the diplomacy needed to work between the different families working in Vegas.   Disgusted, Tony Accardo circumvented Sam Giancana's authority and called Caifano back to Chicago and demoted him to the numbers pool, but, Giancana, almost as an act of defiance, put Caifano under his wing as all around trouble shooter. Once Giancana fell from power in 1964, one of the first orders that Accardo gave was to toss Caifano out of power, forever. By 1965, Caifano, the onetime God of Vegas, was reduced to the status of a neighborhood bookmaker on Chicago's West Side and was warned to keep his mouth shut and his nose clean. He was given enough income from keeping him from going broke, but otherwise he was as out as out could get in mobdom.

*****

Panarella, Charles: AKA Moose, Charlie Moose. Born; January 5, 1922. A Capo in the Colombo Crime family. Legend holds that Panarella had almost a superhuman strength as a young man and once forced another hood to kiss his own testicles by bending him over by the neck before killing him.

In the summer of 2001, law enforcement sources said that Panarella was in New York at a sit down between the Colombo's and the Genovese crime family to solve a dispute over a territorial issue. Panarella can be heard on an Organized Crime Task Force bug bragging about his position within the Colombo crime family and threatening a younger Colombo family member who questioned his authority. In 2003 at age 81, Panarella was indicted for labor racketeering in connection with alleged labor law violations and construction payoffs. The charges were linked to alleged payoffs within the local office of the International Union of Operating Engineers and to fraud associated with the construction of a minor league baseball stadium on Staten Island as well as a Brooklyn post office. Although he was jailed briefly in 1940, he has spent, considering his six decades in the mob, very little time behind bars. Mob legend says that Panarella, whose crew excelled in bank robbery, drug dealing and control of the sheet metal workers union in New York City, ducked several attempts on his life including the Gallo inspired shooting at the Neapolitan Noodle in 1972 when two Chicago businessmen were gunned down by mistake after Panarella and company switched tables with them. In the mid-1980s, Panarella own crew, led by his own brother-in-law John Jackie DeRoss and included mob stars like Wild Bill Cutolo and Greg Scarpa, rebelled against his iron fisted rule and Carmine Junior Persico exiled him to Las Vegas. Persico didn't care about the crews complains but he apparently was concerned that Panarella might aligned himself with the growing power of capo John Sonny Franzese and undermine Persico's leadership role as the feds were bringing charges that would ultimately send him away for good.

When Vic Orena took over, Panarella's fortunes in the family began to rise again and Although he still based his operation in Vegas, he was charged with overseeing the family interests in Brooklyn Locals 14 & 15 of the International Union of Operating Engineers. However, Panarella was added to the Nevada Book of excluded person in 1997 due to his 1994 conviction in a drug money laundering scam involving the Maxim casino in which Panarella was convicted of attempting to launder money through the Maxim as part of a scheme to purchase a farm for $500,000 to $1 million by arranging for profits from illegal drug transactions to be deposited at a cashier's cage at the casino. He served less than 15 months for the crime.

Barred from the casinos or not, that didn't stop Panarella from dropping by the office of Las Vegas Mayor and former mob lawyer Oscar Goodman in 1999. Panarella, Goodman explained, "came up without an appointment and asked whether I could help his son, I tried to." Goodman had just ducked another firestorm several weeks before the Panarella visitation for socializing in his home with Joey Cusumano, another former client and Black Book member. Goodman insisted he did nothing wrong, nor did he see anything wrong with meeting with Panarella and further insisted, remarkably, that he was not aware that Panatela's name is among those in the states Black Book. When reporters asked if Goodman knew Panarella was a mob soldier, Goodman said, "I don't know what that means. I never saw him associated with anyone who was a mobster."

Vincent "Vinnie Ocean" Palermo, the former head of the DeCavalcante crime family who had turned government informant, told the FBI he spotted Panarella leaving Goodman's office in mid-1999. Goodman said that he had never met Palermo. "I never heard of him," Goodman said. "I would remember `Vinnie Ocean' because I would hope he'd jump in it." However, Palermo told the FBI that he made a $10,000 contribution to Goodman's mayoral campaign in 1999 because Goodman told him he would help him with zoning for a proposed topless club in Las Vegas called Queens.

"Goodman told (Palermo) that as soon as he was elected mayor, he would help (Palermo) with the zoning issue," an FBI report stated. Palermo told the FBI he donated $10,000 to Goodman's campaign through a third party. Palermo said that when he returned to Las Vegas after Goodman took office to meet with one of the new mayor's aides, he was waiting in Goodman's office and spotted Panarella and that Panarella "kissed the mayor's assistant on both his cheeks and left."

Goodman became angry when pressed for details of the Panarella meeting and its aftermath. He refused to answer several questions by reporters that he considered inappropriate but explained that "I helped the young man get into the University of San Diego," but when asked whether he was successful in securing a job for Panarella's son, Goodman at first said, "That's none of your business." And when asked if Panarella was a personal friend Goodman screamed at reporters "I'm going to bar you from City Hall if you keep asking questions like that. I'll bar you from City Hall."

*****

Remmer Elmer: AKA Bones (He specialized in burying bodies for the mob, hence the name bones and not, as he claimed, because he gambled with dice) A San Francisco gambler who was the early version of what is now known as a whale in gambling establishments worldwide. Remmer became a public figure when he was mentioned in the Kefauver hearings. He was also an associate of Jimmy Lanza and was the link between Las Vegas and the San Francisco LCN. Remmer "who always had tax troubles," sought to clear up a $7,000 dollar tax deficiency by bribing a chief field director for the internal revenue office in Reno Nevada in 1946. Remmer bought $2,400 dollars' worth of valueless stock in some copper minds that the chief was selling. According to the Kefauver hearing records Remmer wrote the check out to the agent and proceeded to tear up a check for the $7,000 dollars that he owed to the government on the delinquent amount. Following the initial stock purchase the agent then began making yearly trips from Reno to San Francisco to make out the income tax returns of the gambler. At the time of the hearings Remmer had once again fallen behind or failed to pay another $910,000 dollars in taxes for the years 1942-1947. Stubborn to the end Bones refused to pay the amount and was shipped off to prison.

*****

Remo Gaggi: Remo Gaggi was the fictionalized name in the Scorcese film Casino for Chicago boss Joey Aiuppa

*****

Roselli, John: When the Chicago outfit moved in on Hollywood, the only person out west who was truly happy about the move was Johnny Roselli, because finally, after fifteen years of being exiled to the West coast, Roselli's star was starting to shine. Roselli was Chicago's sleeper agent out west, having been sent there in late 1924, to develop gambling, extortion and vice rackets for the outfit, and to help set up a national wire service, which was run by Moses Annenberg, whose family would later publish TV Guide. The outfit's choice (actually it was Al Capone's decision) to send Johnny Roselli to Hollywood was a smart one, because Johnny was a real hustler, an "earner," with movie star good looks, an easy charm and a smooth but phony style that fit right into the Hollywood scene of the fifties and sixties. But despite his polished manner, expensive suits and practiced dialogue, Roselli was nothing more than a slicked-back hood, an antisocial punk with deep, psychological problems that put a permanent chip on his shoulders. Prison doctors labeled him an extreme paranoid.

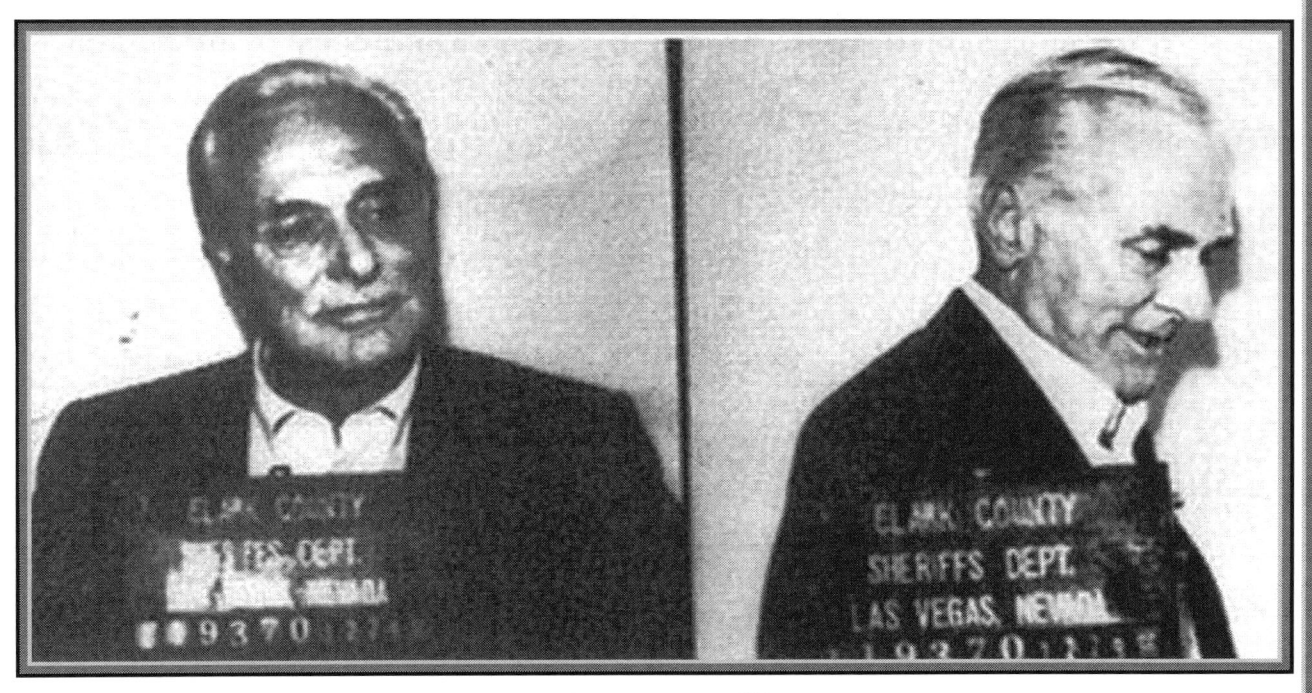

Johnny Roselli

An illegal immigrant into the United States, Roselli always claimed he didn't know his birth date, instead celebrating his birthday on July 4, since it was "easy to remember and comes around at the same time every year." He said he thought he was born in 1905, but he couldn't remember where; it was all a lie of course, because when it came to his personal business, Johnny Roselli lied all the time. Roselli knew exactly when he was born, June 4, 1905, and where he was born, as Filippo Sacco in Esteria, Italy. He came to Boston, illegally, when he was 6 years old. His first brush with the law came on September 14, 1922, when Roselli was trailed by federal narcotic agents as he delivered a quarter ounce bag of morphine to a drug addict named Fisher who was also a government informant. Roselli was arrested, but made bail. The case was eventually dropped because the state's witness, Fisher, had disappeared and was believed to have been killed.   He was also an arsonist. After his drug arrest, Roselli and his step father, hoping to finance a trip back to their native Italy tried to burn their house down to collect on the fire insurance but the Fire Department reacted too quickly and put the fire out. After that, Roselli went to New York and started running bootleg booze and acting as a guard, protecting beer wagons as they rolled through the streets of Manhattan.   It was at that point, probably in or about the middle of 1923that Roselli was recruited out to Chicago by the Capone organization which was in the middle of yet another territory war. Likable, smart and handsome, Roselli eventually managed to get close to Al Capone's inner circle, at one point he was even reported to be Capone's cousin, which is how other hoods explained the relationship, but the connection may have been Roselli's ability to provide Capone with a steady flow of cocaine out of New York.

 While in Chicago, Roselli leafed through an encyclopedia and found the name Cosimo Roselli, a fifteenth-century painter who contributed frescoes of Moses on Mount Sinai and the Last Super on the walls of the Sistine Chapel. Impressed, and in need of a new name anyway, Roselli kept his first name, John, and took on the last name, Roselli.

Eventually Capone shared his lifelong dream with Roselli, to move west to Los Angeles, then still a mostly rural but growing community, and rebuild the mob out there. Roselli had always wanted to move to California, in fact when he was a boy he had dreams of settling their with his mother, so when Johnny Torrio, the leader of the Chicago outfit in 1925, and Al Capone, talked to Roselli about spearheading their move out west, Johnny was all for it. Roselli's first two years out west were rough. He was sick and gaunt from tuberculosis, and penniless since all that the Chicago outfit had going out in California were high hopes and big plans, but no money producing operations. Then, in 1926, Roselli went to work for Anthony "The Hat" Cornero a colorful if slightly off-balance southern California bootlegger and gambler.

While it lasted, Cornero has an amazing life. Born Anthony Cornero Stralla in an Italian village near the Swiss boarder in 1895, the Cornero family had owned a large farm there but his father lost it in a card game.

More bad luck came when young Tony Cornero accidentally set fire to the family harvest, driving them broke and forcing them to emigrate to San Francisco in the early 1900s.

At age 16, Tony pleaded guilty to robbery and did ten months in reform school, he moved to southern California and racked up another ten arrest in ten years which included three for bootlegging and three for attempted murder.

He was ambitious, but as late as 1922, Cornero was still driving a cab before he decided to branch off into the rum running business. He started with a string of small boats and smuggled high priced whisky over the Canadian border and sold it to the wealthy and better clubs in Los Angles. At the same time, Cornero ran rum from Mexico to Los Angles, his freighters easily avoiding the understaffed coast guard.

Tony the Hat Cornero

Next, Tony purchased the merchant ship, the SS Lily, which he stocked with 4,000 cases of the best booze money could buy and ran the booze into Los Angles under moonlight. In 1931, Cornero decided to switch over to gambling and moved, with his brothers, to Las Vegas and opened one of the town's first larger casinos, the Green Meadows, which was known for its staff of attractive and friendly waitresses.

The Meadows

Tony Cornero sits in the left front of the photo

The Meadows turned a small, but healthy profit, and soon Cornero was investing his returns into other casinos in the state, mostly in Las Vegas.

The money started to pour in, and before long, New York's Luciano, Lansky, Frank Costello sent around their representatives and demanded a cut in Cornero's action, but Cornero, who had always operated on the fringe of the national syndicate, refused to pay. Instead he had built up his own organization and was strong enough to turn the syndicate bosses down. The Syndicate, which had a small but powerful presence on the West coast, prepared for war and started by burning Cornero's Green Meadows casino to the ground. Realizing he could never win the fight, Cornero sold out his interest in Nevada and returned to Los Angles.

In 1938 Cornero bought several large ships and refurbished them into luxury casino's at a cost of over $300,000, and anchored them three miles off the coast of Santa Monica and had gamblers shuttled from shore by way of motor boats.

Cornero's lead ship, The Rex, had a crew of 350, waiters' waitresses, cooks, a full orchestra, and enforcers. The first class dining room served French cuisine only and on most nights, some 2,000 patrons flooded on to the ship to gamble, dance and drink the night away.

Tony was hauling in an estimated $300,000 a night after expenses, and the money would have continued to pour in, had he not become the center of a reform movement in Los Angeles County.

State Attorney General Earl Warren ordered a raid on the Rex and several other of Cornero's off coast ships.

Cornero's ship The Rex

Cornero and the California government fought a series of battles, with Tony's lawyers arguing that his ships were operating in international waters, and the California government taking the indefensible stance that it didn't care where they were they were, they were still illegal.

Back and forth it went, until at one point, after raiders had smashed almost a half a million worth of gambling equipment on one of his ships, Cornero decided to fight back. When the law men came to raid his ships, Cornero ordered his men to repel the attackers with water hoses. A sea battle went on for nine hours and the lawmen finally gave up.

But Cornero was beaten and he knew it and he closed up his off shore operations.

Tony tried to open a few gambling joints inside Los Angles, but Mickey Cohen, the ruling bookie and dope dealer in the town, shut him down. When Cornero refused to back down, Cohen had his boys bomb Cornero's Beverly Hills estate. Fearing for his life, Cornero took his fortune and moved to Las Vegas.

After several years in Vegas, Cornero undertook his dream, to build the largest gambling casino-hotel in the world, the Stardust. Then he went broke.

Tony went out like the gambler he was. Of the estimated $25 million he had earned his career as a gambler, Tony Cornero had less than $800 in his pockets when he choked.

But before that, Prohibition had made Cornero rich and Roselli profited as a result. For the first time in his life, Roselli had enough money to rent a house outside of the Italian ghettos he had known since moving to America. He bought a car, started to dress better, and, as the bootlegger and bookmaker to a growing number of movie stars, he started to move in higher circles.

It was Cornero who recommended Roselli to Longy Zwillman, the New Jersey labor rackets boss who had expanded his criminal empire into the most successful rum-running enterprise on the East coast. Zwillman was a Hollywood regular and met with Roselli often, grew to like him and came to rely on him as his primary West coast contact and even assigned Roselli to watch over the various starlets that Zwillman dated. In turn, Zwillman put other big name East coast hoods in touch with Roselli as the man to see when they went west, and when Capone traveled to Los Angeles in 1927, Roselli showed him around the city and introduced him to movie stars, which impressed the movie stars and Capone, and gave Roselli a lot of prestige around town.

Roselli also remembered Capone's visit and talked about it often over the years. He said that even for California's laid-back lifestyle of the twenties, Capone's banana yellow suits and shocking pink silk shoes, "pimp gear" he called it, were outrageous. He remembered that the press, crowds and the police hounded them everywhere and Capone seemed to love all the attention. Roselli would remember it for the rest of his life and the smart crook that he was, he learned from it. He shunned Capone's type of flamboyance. He learned to fit in with the Hollywood crowd, but to keep a low profile, and aside from an arrest in Los Angeles in 1925 for carrying a concealed weapon, Roselli was virtually unknown to law enforcement.

After Capone went to jail, Roselli was still out in Los Angeles, exiled as he saw it, and considering a career in films. Then Frank Nitti called and told Johnny that his moment had come, the outfit was moving in on Hollywood and Roselli would lead the attack on the West Coast, the so-called Bioff scandal, that extorted millions out of the Hollywood studios in the mid-1930s. Convicted in scam, Roselli did a few years hard time and strutted out of jail on August 13, 1947.

The slick little hood leaped right back into the rackets and the center of Hollywood. Even while he was in prison, Roselli kept in touch with the Hollywood community by way of his friend, talent agent Danny Winkler, who wrote to him with the latest gossip, and from the 250 letters he received from a bit-part actress named Beatrice Ann Frank, who, in 1947, became Roselli's fiancée, but nothing ever came of it. Eventually, Johnny did marry a promising young actress named June Lang, born June Valasek, who was 12 years younger than Roselli, was madly in love with him and had no idea that he was a gangster, because Roselli had told her he was an aspiring movie producer. But, with time, the truth came out, and Johnny promised her he would leave the rackets. But what he said, and what he did were two different things and soon, Lang came to see that Roselli would never change and divorced him.

After that, Johnny dated actresses Betty Hutton, Lana Turner and Donna Reed, among many others, and still managed to find time to have an affair with Bugsy Siegel's girlfriend, Virginia Hill, but that may have been ordered by Paul Ricca back in Chicago, so that Hill and Roselli would spy on each other. Amazingly, producer Joe Schenck, just out of prison himself as a result of the Bioff mess, sponsored Roselli for a job at Eagle Lion Studios, a small, British owned production company, where the hood worked with Brian Foy, Vice President in charge of production. Eagle-Lion churned out a dozen true life, fast paced, low budget crime related semi-documentary films, which Foy clipped out of the tabloid papers. The Docudramas were popular with critics and fans alike, and lead the way for television police dramas like Dragnet.

Roselli would work at Eagle Lion, on the records anyway, as a purchasing agent for $50 a week and would be "promoted," by Foy of course, through the ranks, to associate producer. It was the only legitimate job Roselli ever had and apparently he had a knack for the business, and produced several hit films for Eagle-Lion, including the dark gangster dramas, which now have a cult status, "He Walked By Night," "T-Men," and "Canon City."

Roselli's other official source of income, outside of the Studios, was as an agent for Nationwide, the only wire service into California and wholly owned and operated by the mob, although he was supplementing his income by replacing Willie Bioff as the DuPont Film Corporation's representative to Hollywood. Actually, Roselli probably knew nothing at all about film stock, but the outfit still controlled large parts of the studios and if DuPont wanted to remain a dominant force in Hollywood, it had to cooperate and leave Roselli on the payroll. DuPont never complained since Roselli had so much influence with the studio bosses and the company wanted to take the Hollywood film market from Eastman-Kodak, who had a virtual lock on the market.

Roselli was also the Chicago outfit's West Coast executioner of choice, and since territory battles for control of Los Angeles continued on into the early 1970s, Roselli did, as Jimmy "The Weasel" Fratianno, an LA mob boss turned informant said, "a lot of work when he was a kid. He did a lot of fuck'n work, don't worry." Otherwise, Roselli kept his standard low profile and shunned publicity. But, flush with cash, Roselli allowed himself one little bit of color, he moved into Hollywood's famous Garden of Allah, then a swinging bungalow complex that was home to dozens of stars, from Humphreys Bogart to Edward G. Robinson. But Roselli's move into the heart of stardom was no mistake either.

Johnny was also one of Hollywood's leading loan sharks, was ordered by Chicago to spread out as much mob influence among the stars and the people who ran the studios as he could, either with money or drugs, and since most of the big stars were constantly overspending themselves, his loan sharking business grew at phenomenal rates. Over three decades, Roselli estimated that he had loaned out at least five million dollars in cash to some of Hollywood's leading stars and producers, from Ronald Reagan to Ed Sullivan and dozens of others.

Roselli was also the Chicago outfit's talent scout, finding promising actresses or actors, and then sponsoring their careers in Tinseltowns. According to Johnny, it was the Chicago outfit that sponsored the Marx Brothers, George Raft, Jimmy Durante, Marie McDonald, Clark Gable, Gary Cooper, Jean Harlow, Gary Grant and Wendy Barrie and as a result were awarded extravagant contracts by the studios. The next logical step was to control the talent outlets, so in the late 1940s, when the mob's Vegas casinos discovered that live entertainment brought in the crowds, Roselli and the mob opened a talent booking agency called Monte Prosser Productions, which was the only agency used by all Vegas casinos. Roselli ran the company of his apartment at the Desert Inn, and had such a firm grip on Vegas' entertainment, that he even had the contract to represent the company that put the ice machine in all the hotels.

Roselli and Foy, despite Foy's financial success at Eagle-Lion studios, were both let go because of Foy's brash, confrontational style that annoyed the studio brass, and when his three-year contract expired in 1950 he was released and Roselli was booted out with him. Foy bounced over to Warner Brothers studios but couldn't take Roselli with him since the studio had, officially anyway, barred Johnny from the lot. But Foy remained close with Roselli: "They were like the Rover boys," Foy's niece said, "they went everywhere together."

The pair spent most of their weekends at Foy's house, where there was also a party. At one of those weekend parties, Foy introduced Roselli to one of his favorite contract players at Warner, Bill Campbell, who lived in the same apartment complex as Roselli. Campbell was married to a stunning young actress named Judy Campbell, who was born Judith Eileen Katherine Immoor in Pacific Palisades in 1934. She had met Campbell when she was 16, and married him two years later in 1952. Bill Campbell became fast friends and Campbell introduced Roselli to his wife. Like most men who met her, Roselli was awestruck at Campbell's beauty and taken with her quick wit and disarming charm. After Judy divorced Campbell in 1954, Roselli introduced Judy to Frank Sinatra in late 1959 and a year later, Sinatra introduced Campbell to both John Kennedy and Mob Boss Sam Giancana.

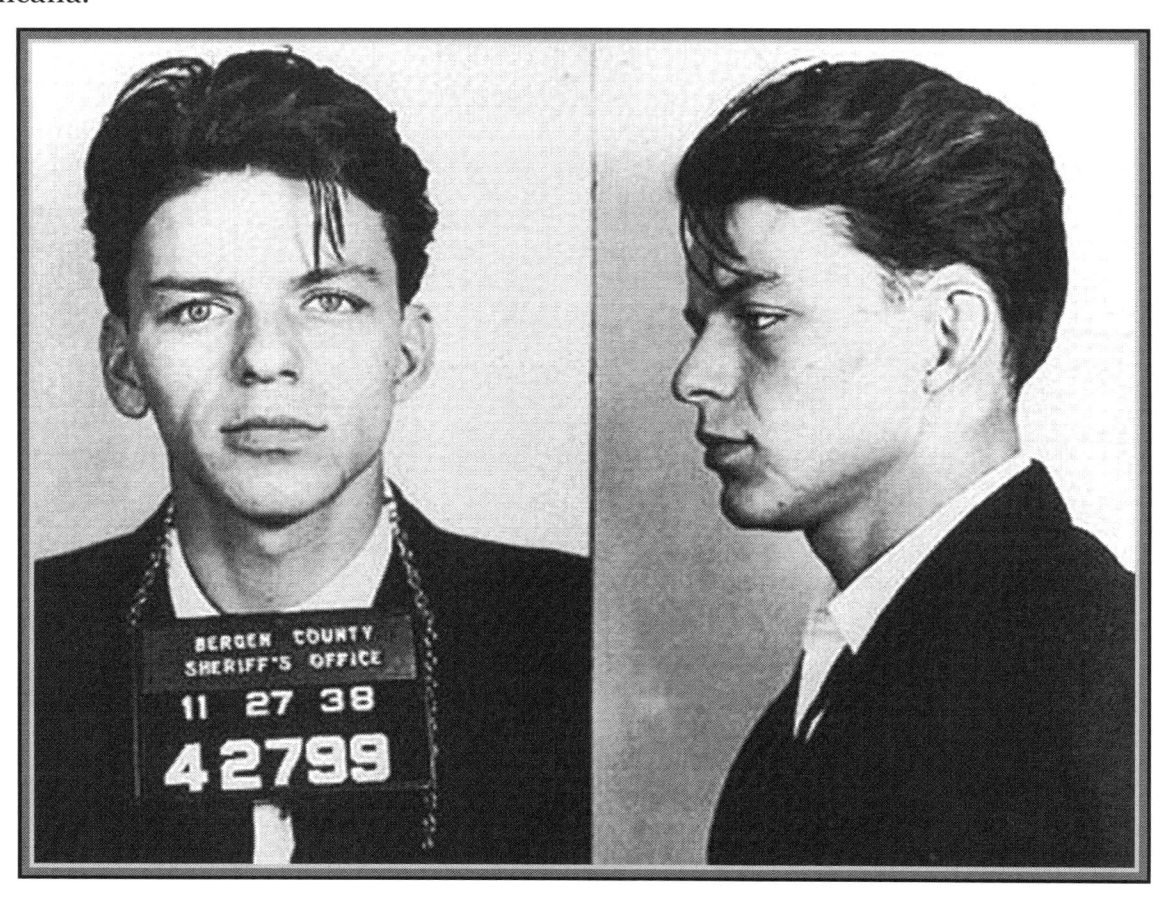

Sinatra

It was about this same time, in 1960-61, that Roselli became embroiled in the Mafia-CIA-White House plots to kill Cuba's Castro. It was interesting that one day in early 1975, film producer Bernie Foy called Johnny Roselli with the idea of doing a remake of the movie "The Exorcist." In the new version, a nun would be possessed by the devil who would then drive her to acts of sexual depravity. Roselli read the script, but rejected it as sacrilegious. However, Roselli then pitched his own idea for a film. The story concerned a patriotic mobster who becomes entangled in a White House-CIA plot to assassinate Fidel Castro. However, the scheme backfired when Castro hires his own mobsters to kill the American President. Foy and his financial backers heard out the Roselli pitch and then rejected it as too implausible.

In 1966, Johnny Roselli arranged for St. Louis Mafia Don Anthony Giordano and the caporegime in Detroit, Anthony Zerilli, to buy hidden assets in the Frontier Hotel. It was an otherwise uneventful, commonplace underworld deal. Johnny collected his $100,000 finder fee and that was the end of it. Then a Federal grand jury called Roselli in for questioning about his years in Las Vegas. Roselli refused to testify on the grounds that he could incriminate himself, so the grand jury gave him immunity, and Roselli talked, although in the end, he really didn't give the jury anything against anybody. Unfortunately for Roselli, his testimony was stamped secret, so when Giordano and Zerilli were convicted of hiding their assets in the Frontier Hotel, the sale that Roselli had arranged, it looked like Johnny had talked. After that, he was a dead man. But before anything could be done, Roselli and four others were indicted for running a card cheating hustle at the Friars Club in Beverly Hills, where Roselli was a member, having been sponsored by the club's founder, Georgie Jessel, Dean Martin, and, of course, Frank Sinatra.

Roselli thanked them by setting up a high stakes gin rummy game that included Phil Silvers, Zeppo Marx, and Tony Martin, the millionaire husband to Debbi Reynolds. Unknown to them Roselli had a "peeper" hidden behind a wall at the tables who transmitted the players' hands electronically to Roselli. When the scam was exposed, one of Roselli's spotters in the game, George Sears, turned informant. Roselli was arrested, found guilty and sentenced to five years at McNeil Island. In the meantime, the Organized Crime Unit within the Justice Department was planning to have him deported if he didn't start talking about his life in the outfit. This time Roselli talked. He was released from prison, but he was broke and borrowing money to get by and in the last half of 1974, he was forced to move into his sister's house in Florida and that's where they caught up with him. Johnny Roselli was last seen in the company of the two men getting aboard a private yacht for a cruise. As he sat on the deck sipping a drink, one of the men slipped behind him and choked him to death with a white nylon rope. Then they taped a washcloth over his mouth, sawed off his legs at the thigh with a hand saw, stuffed him into a 55 gallon drum that was weighed down with chains.

The coroner figured that the killer also shot him and then decided to dig the bullet out of his body before they dumped him in the barrel and then dumped it into the bay. Body gases pushed the body onto the surface ten days later. Several weeks later, during a meeting with the boys, Chicago's acting boss, Joey Auippa summed up the measure of Roselli's life with the outfit: "You remember that guy from the old days, that guy ... what the fuck was his name ... that guy they found in the barrel down there inside of Florida? What do you think of that?" There was a moment's silence until somebody across the room cracked, "Johnny in a drum."

*****

Sachs-Tobman: In the 1980s, Al Sachs,(1926-2002) a gambler and Herb Tobman, (1925-2006) a business investor, took over the mobbed owned and troubled Stardust hotel-casino. The previous management, Allan Glick and Lefty Rosenthal were booted out by the government due to their ties with the Cleveland and Chicago Mafia. Sachs had been around the casinos since the 1940s when he worked as a dealer for the Chicago Outfits big dollar poker games held in the then Jewish neighborhood on the West Side, the games were supervised by Lenny Yaras and Lenny Patrick. He had also worked as a manager in the Havana casino, pre-Castro. In 1955, he opened the Royal Nevada casino (Which became the Stardust hotel). In 1958, he was a minor investor in the very mobbed -up Tropicana. He returned to the Stardust in the early 1970s but argued with Alan Glick and left to become the manager of the Aladdin in 1977. Herbie Tobman, who worked as a Catskill Mountains resort bellhop and later as a Las Vegas gas station attendant in his late 20s, was a real estate investor, furniture store, cab company and diner operator. In the 1950s, he was the general manager of the Moulin Rouge casino, the first racially integrated casino in the state of Nevada. In 1971, he became the general manager of the Aladdin casino.

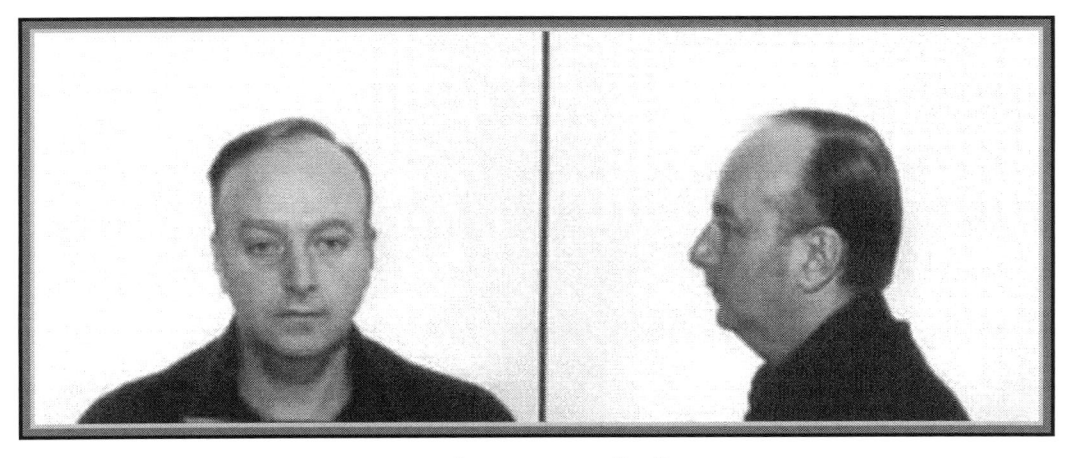

Lefty Rosenthal

The problem with Sachs and Tobman was, that no matter what casino they managed, money seemed to disappear from the count room although they denied, loudly and often, that they allowed the Mafia to skim from the casinos and that they were little more than figure heads. In 1979, the partners formed Trans-Sterling Corporation to take over the Stardust. At about the same time, Joe Yablonsky became special agent in charge of the Las Vegas FBI office. One morning Yablonsky and a junior agent were having coffee in the Riviera casino coffee shop when Yablonsky spied Herb Tobman across the room talking to Mobster Moe Dalitz and his partner Morris Kleinman. On the way out, Tobman stopped at Yablonsky's table and good naturedly put his arm on the junior FBI agent and, nodding to Yablonsky said I guess you don't mind who you're seen with. "It was intended to be a joke but Yablonsky failed to see the humor. He declared war on Tobman and Sachs by opening a standing investigation into their dealings, which included charges of skimming from the Fremont and the Stardust. The investigation went on for four years. The investigation had its awkward moments. Yablonsky, who was Jewish, joined the Temple Beth Shalom where Dalitz and Tobman were regular worshippers. By 1984, Sachs and Tobman were tossed out of casino business by allegations of skimming and were fined a record $3 million as part of the agreement to surrender ownership of the Stardust and their gaming licenses.

*****

San Francisco Mob   Francesco Lanza was the first Mafia boss in San Francisco, shooting his way to the top during prohibition. Between April 28, 1928 and May 18, 1932, Lanza either murdered or ordered the murders of independent bootleggers Jerry Feri, Alfredo Scariso, Mario Filippi, Frank Boca, Genaro Broccolo and Luigi Malvese. When the bloodletting ended, the independents were out of business and Lanza ruled supreme. Lanza operated the famous Fisherman's Warf with his business partner, Giuseppe Alioto On July 14, 1937 Lanza died of natural causes. His son, Joseph, would later become boss over the San Francisco rackets. Anthony J. Lima succeeded Frank Lanza as boss over the San Francisco rackets in 1937. Lima is believed to have ordered his underboss Michael Abati to murder Chicago gangster Nick DeJohn. Both were arrested but eventually the charges were dismissed. On April 27, 1953 Lima was sentenced to the California State Prison for grand theft. He never returned to power.

   Michael Abati ruled as boss of San Francisco from 1953-1961, succeeding Tony Lima. He attended the mob summit at Apalachin in November 1957 with his underboss Joseph Lanza. Abati was one of the hoods held by police after the meeting was raided. The intense focus from law enforcement and the press resulted in further investigations into his activities. As a result of this he was deported back to Italy on July 8, 1961. He died of natural causes on September 5, 1962.   Joseph Lanza AKA "Jimmy" was probably the most successful Mafia boss that the San Francisco family has ever had. He ruled from 1961 through 1989. Under his reign, the family grew in size and in wealth and Lanza expanded the family's holdings to include interests in Nevada where William "Bones' Remmer represented him.   Lanza was also connected to mob bosses Joe Cerrito of San Jose and Joseph Civello of Dallas. His underboss, Gaspare "Bill" Sciortino, was the first cousin to the underboss of the Los Angeles Samuel Sciortino.   Lanza was believed to have given permission for the murder of former New England family associate, turned government witness. Joseph "The Animal" Barboza. In 1976. Lanza died on June 19, 1989 from natural causes at the age of 73.   At the close of the 20th century the US Justice Department claimed that Frank Velotta AKA "Skinny" was underboss or possible boss of the tiny San Francisco family. A former burglar and associate of Jimmy Frattiano, his underboss is suspected to be Angelo Commito.

*****

San Jose. San Diego Mob: It's generally agreed that the first boss over the San Jose, California rackets was Onofrio Sciortino. By 1942, Sciortino controlled the areas loan sharking, gambling and prostitution. When he died of natural causes on September 10, 1959, leadership fell to his underboss Joseph Cerrito. An Italian immigrant, Cerrito arrived to the states from Sicily in the 1920s. He is believed to have moved into the San Jose area in the early 1940s. He was one of the Mafia bosses caught in the November 1957 Apalachin Summit raid. In October of 1964 Cerrito was identified meeting with Bonanno family former Consiglieri Frank Garofalo at a hotel in Palermo, Sicily. Authorities speculate they were discussing the ensuing war within the Bonanno crime family, the so-called "Banana War". Cerrito died on September 8, 1978 from natural causes. Capo Angelo Marino who had close ties to San Francisco mayor Joseph Alioto throughout the late 1960s and early 1970s took his place. He was also close to San Francisco boss James "Jimmy" Lanza, Consiglieri to the Los Angeles Mob. Marino owned the California Cheese Company, which controlled 85% of the cheese distribution in California and 50% west of the Mississippi River. In October 1977 Marino and his son were indicted for the murder of father and son, Orlando and Peter Catelli. Apparently Peter Catelli had attempted to obtain a job with Marino's company. When Marino refused to hire him Catelli attempted to extort $100,000 from Marino, who then ordered Catelli's father to kill him. The father refused and both were shot. However the father survived the ordeal and agreed to testify for the prosecution. Marino, under the guise of bad health, avoided going to trial for the three years while at the same time continuing to operate his family. On October 12, 1980 Marino was convicted of second-degree murder and attempted murder. The conviction was later overturned on appeals and he was released. Marino died of a heart attack in February of 1983. Emmanuel Joseph Figlia took Marino's place in the organization however there is very little left for the Mafia to control in the San Jose area. Asian and Russian gangsters have moved in strength and now command much of the illegal rackets there.

*****

Sands Casino: Jimmy Blue Eyes Alo rolled his new Cadillac carefully down the wide open coastal road to Hallendale, swerving to avoid the occasional gigantic wave that crashed and spilled over onto the blacktop and driving slowly around the shells of the huge land crabs that seemed big enough to puncture a car's tires. A city boy, born and raised in the hell holes of New York's Lower East Side, Jimmy Blue Eyes wasn't used to all the nature of the still rugged Florida coastline, but he loved it. He loved every clean and uncluttered foot of it, the salt smell of the ocean, the long open blue skies. He had already decided that this was where he would rebuild his life.

A decade before Jimmy had strolled out of Sing Sing prison after a three stint for robbery. He did his time right. He never ratted on his friends. To his credit, Alo never made excuses about his time behind bars. He did the crime. He served the time and he was sorry that the whole thing had happened. When he walked out of prison in 1926, he was Made in the Mafia and went to work under "Joe the Boss" Masseria, one of the old-fashioned Mafia bosses, the "Mustache Petes," who ruled the Mafia in the new world as though they had never left the old world.

Alo was the Mafia muscle behind Meyer Lansky, the mob's financial genius, and although his power reached from Manhattan's crowded boulevards, to the sun-drenched beaches of Cuba, to the glitter of Vegas and Hollywood, few people have ever heard of Jimmy Blue Eyes Alo. In fact, if it had not been for Francis Ford Coppola's nod to Alo's legend in the film The Godfather Part 2, where Alo is portrayed as Johnny Ola, or Alo spelled backwards, the Sicilian messenger boy for Hyman Roth, Alo's name would be forever forgotten, and Jimmy Blue Eyes would have preferred it that way.

Despite the senseless brutality that was his life, Alo exuded an aura of wisdom and kindness. People felt comfortable around him, drawn to him for guidance. "There was," wrote Robert Lacey, "something pastoral, almost monkish, about him." When the film director John Houston met Alo in the 1960s, when Houston was filming his epic The Bible, in which Alo and others from his world had a financial interest, Huston "was not entirely joking when he lobbied Alo to play the role of God."

Of course, in a sense, he did play God. It was Alo, who, in 1949, ordered the powerful William Morris agency, owned in part by Alo and other New York mobsters, to give Marilyn Monroe an exclusive contract, which was almost a guarantee to success in the motion picture industry. Johnny Roselli said that it was he who called Jimmy Blue Eyes and asked him to place Monroe under contract, because Roselli had been ordered by his boss, Tony Accardo, to "find somebody" for the mob to groom and invest in. Roselli said he found Monroe. And it was Jimmy Blue Eyes who, in 1938, discovered Hallandale Florida and its dozens of hidden casinos that were money machines for the independent gamblers who ran them. Alo liked what he saw, and understood its potential, but he knew that in order to make Hallandale work for the outfit, he would need a gambler to watch the casino floors, a manager to keep the books and big cash to get the joints off the ground.

Jimmy Alo wasn't a gambler or a manager, and his money, although he had a lot of it, was out on the street. He would need a partner and there was no question who that would be, Alo's old friend from back in New York, Meyer Lansky. Lansky and Alo had met back in 1929, when Charlie Luciano called Jimmy Blue Eyes to his apartment high up in the Barbizon Plaza Hotel on Central Park west, and told Alo that he wanted him to guard Lansky, that there might be a war ahead of them and Luciano would need Lansky's money making abilities in the event they had to hit the guns.

They liked each other from the start. Small men, just under five foot three inches tall, and only a year apart in their ages, Alo and Lansky were both basically shy men who had crawled out of the almost unbelievable poverty of New York's slums. They were book loving, low profile, chain-smokers, without much to say to those they didn't know and they were both obsessed with obtaining at least a veneer of respectability. Unlike Meyer, who never did any serious jail time, Alo had done a three-year stretch up to Sing Sing prison for armed robbery. But, he did his time right, he never ratted on his friends and when he walked out of jail in 1926, he was a Made guy working under "Joe the Boss" Masseria. Lanksy liked Alo's idea of building a new life in Florida and poured his considerable energies, talent and cash into two massive casinos, the Plantation and the Colonial Inn.

Business boomed, and where success goes, others follow and by 1948, Hallandale was "a gamblers paradise … a little Las Vegas before its time." With the money they made from the Hallandale operations, Lansky and Alo founded the Emby Distributing Company which had a lock on the distribution of jukeboxes and cigarette vending machines in the lucrative greater New York area. Emby jukeboxes gave Lansky and Alo control of the popular music outlets during the 1940s in the massive New York market, and to no small degree Frank Sinatra's amazing career took off as a result of the hoods' control of what records appeared in their jukeboxes.

Unfortunately for Sinatra, Alo's boss, Frank Costello was also pressing bootleg copies, millions of them, of Sinatra's records and selling them from record store outlets. Then, corporate officers at Wurlitzer realized who Lansky and Alo were and asked Lansky, the group's front man, to sell out his routes. "They said I was a bad risk for them," Lansky said later, and without trouble, he and the others sold off their Juke Box routes to outside investors. With the cash Lansky and Alo made from the sale of Embry, they invested in a corporation called Consolidated Television with $15,000, owning about 10% of the company. But the gangsters weren't able to see or understand the big picture behind television, and in late 1949 they withdrew from the business.

 By 1950, Meyer and Alo were rich and, miles and worlds away from the bloodletting of the street rackets in New York and Chicago. They started to enjoy their role as the enlightened men of reason and logic within the mob and they always went out of their way to make sure that the newspaper people and the law understood that they were gamblers, and not tied in with "the rough stuff", as Meyer called it, prostitution, loan sharking and, most importantly, murder.   And while it was true that they didn't deal in those realms themselves, they had no aversion to dealing with men who did, and they both understood that in the underworld, murder was an option. Beginning in 1952, Alo began to spend half of his time in Vegas, looking after his and Lansky's investments there, and settling one dispute after another.   In 1967, after Meyer Lansky beat yet another federal assault, the government went after his closest friend, Jimmy Alo, and charged him with a 72-count indictment involving securities fraud, a scam that Alo had little or nothing to do with. he was found not guilty and retired to Florida.

Now, in 1951 Alo was tired beyond his years. He wanted to rebuild his life and Florida, as foreign to him as another universe, beckoned. Another hood who found his way south to fulfill Young's dream was Julian Kaufman, although everybody in the underworld knew him simply as "Potatoes." Kaufman was a Chicagoan on the run from Al Capone. He had started his criminal career as a fence for stolen mail loot before he learned that gambling offered twice the profit at half the risk. Working on Chicago's North Side, by 1923, Kaufman, along with his sometime partner Dion O'Bannion, was enough of an underworld power to receive an engraved invitation from Johnny Torrio, boss of the Chicago mob, to the funeral of Torrio's top gunner, Frank Capone, brother to Al Capone, who had been gunned down by police during the mob takeover of the city of Cicero. Three years later, he was still a power in the Windy City, no small thing considering the turnover in the business, and he held enough financial interest, in the O'Bannion gang, to be invited to the Hotel Sherman Treaty on October 26 of that year. The peace treaty was called between Chicago's gang leaders after the Capone's gunned down the O'Bannion gang's leader, Hymie Weiss, elevating Schemer Drucci into the gang's leadership position. By 1931, Drucci was dead, shot to death by police in the back seat of a squad car while on his way to jail. Following him to the gang's leadership was the highly incompetent Bugs Moran.

Kaufman and Moran operated the ritziest casino in the city, if not in the entire country, the Sheridan Wave Tournament Club. Admission to the club was by invitation only and uniformed waiters and doorman catered to the customers' every need, including free food, drink and women. It was worth it. Each night the club cleared at least $10,000, of which Bugs Moran took 25% for protection and the police took an additional 10% through their bagman, newspaper leg man Jake Lingle, a cocky runt with direct ties to his childhood friend, the Chief of Police.

After a change of administrations at city hall, and with a decline of the power of the Moran gang, the club was raided in 1929 and locked up for two years. Then, Moran and Kaufman, backed up with a hefty cash investment from super pimp Jake Zuta, decided to reopen the club and sent out engraved invitations to their old clientele. It was at that point that Jake Lingle reappeared demanding a 50% cut on the club's take. When Moran and Kaufman refused, Lingle told them, "If this joint is opened, you'll see more squad cars in front, ready to raid it than you's two ever seen before in your life." Several days later, as Jake Lingle was strolling through a sidewalk underpass, Leo, a professional killer with ties to labor corruption, walked up behind Lingle, pointed a pistol at the back of his head and fired off a round that tore through Lingle's skull and poured his brains out on to the sidewalk, and then calmly walked away.

The murder created sensational headlines in Chicago and the Chicago Tribune, Lingle's newspaper, offered a $55,000 reward for information leading to the arrest and conviction of his killer. That, with the public's outrage at the killing, caused a police crackdown on all of the city's gangs, with some 700 known felons being dragged into police headquarters for questioning. Al Capone, who suffered the most from the crackdown, decided that somebody had to pay for Lingle's killing and all the aggravation it caused, and Moran, Kaufman and Zuta were the mob's first targets.

 Jake Zuta was the first to go. On August 1, 1930, Zuta was hiding out at the Lake View Hotel on the shores of Lake Nemahbin, a summer resort near Delafield, Wisconsin. He had registered under the name Goodman and was known to the staff as big tipper. It was a busy night at the Hotel, couples were swimming in the lake just below the hotel, the beach under the bar was crowded and couples were jam-packed into the Hotel ballroom, and dancing to a local orchestra.

Zuta was the life of the party: "Every time she stops the nearest one will feed her a nickel, let's go, this is the life!" Zuta was in the main lobby dropping nickels into a player piano when seven men walked in. The leader was carrying a machine gun under his arm, the other men were armed with rifles, shotguns and several pistols. They disarmed the doorman Joe Selby. At that very second, Zuta walked past them to make change, and then walked back to the jukebox. The hit men stepped into front of the piano where Zuta had his back turned and lined up firing squad style, and called "Hey Jake!" Zuta turned, half smiling and they opened up on him as the piano played a song called, "It may be good for you but it's bad for me" from a popular musical of the day, "Flying High." One of the gunmen grabbed Zuta by the shoulder as he fell to the floor. He picked him and dragged his dead body to a corner and put him in a chair, and then wordlessly, he was machine gunned twenty-eight bullets in him. As the killers left, one of them turned and said to the dancer, "Don't come out of this place or we starts shooting."

Desperate to save his own life, Kaufman fled to New York and fell under the paid protection of Vincent Alo, AKA Jimmy Blue Eyes. As a Made member of the Mafia (most of Capone's people weren't), Alo was untouchable by the Chicago outfit, and his word was final; as long as Kaufman paid Alo for his protection, he stayed alive. By 1936, Al Capone was in jail, Frank Nitti was running Chicago, the Lingle incident was ancient history and Potatoes Kaufman thought it safe to move out of New York, but not safe enough to return to Chicago. Instead, he headed south and discovered Broward County, and Hallendale, Florida. Back then, Hallandale's main source of income came from the fruit pickers who flooded into the area during the harvest months and holed up at the local boarding house, a rundown shack called the Collins Hotel that rented rooms for a dollar a night, less for weekly guests. Kaufman saw the potential anyway and quickly struck up a partnership with a bookie named Claude Litteral, who had the outlet for the local wire service. Litteral, who was missing an arm, was better known in the area as, "The one armed Bandit."

Kaufman and Litteral ran the wire service and bookmaking operation out of a large tomato packing shed and over time, moved in a roulette wheel and a few crap tables and a bingo parlor. Business boomed and Kaufman added other extras, including a name for the place, The Plantation, taken from a top notch casino that Al Capone had run on the Indiana-Illinois line, back in the roaring twenties. Adding to the pot, was the fact that Hallendale City officials, desperate for income, were willing often to look the other way, not ask too many questions, and bend the law in Kaufman's favor if needed.

Jimmy Blue Eyes knew that Kaufman's Plantation, as successful as it was, was already a creature of the past. What America wanted now were "carpet joints," the new breed of casino that separated itself from the smelly, crowded, inner city gambling houses by embellishments, uniformed doormen, a restaurant and Black Hat chef, and of course, carpeting. Carpet joints were the wave of the future, it was what Americans, flush with cash and ready for fun, wanted. A clean, safe place to spend an evening out on the town, enjoying good food, a floor show and gambling. A dozen of them already dotted the growing suburban towns outside of New York, and with Florida quickly becoming the number one vacation destination of North America, it was just a matter of time before Broward was flooded with the places. But even if the Plantation wasn't a carpet joint, Jimmy Blue Eyes liked what he saw. He understood its potential but he also understood that in order to make the Hallendale deal work, Alo knew he would need a gambler to run the casino floor, a manager to keep the books and big cash to get the joint off the ground. Alo wasn't a gambler by career or a manager by nature and his money, although he had a lot of it, was out on the street. He would need a partner and there was no question who that would be, Alo's old friend from back in New York, Meyer Lansky. Lansky has already earned a reputation for being scrupulously honest, a wise choice on his part, considering whose money he was handling and he and Alo were close. Ann Lansky, Esther Siegel and Flo Alo all used the same interior decorator and dropped small fortunes on Fifth and Madison Avenues shopping district together.

Lansky and Alo had met back in 1929, when Charlie Luciano called Jimmy Blue Eyes to his apartment high up in the Barbizon Plaza Hotel on Central Park West, and told Alo that he wanted him to guard Lansky, that there might be a street war, and Luciano would need Lansky's money-making abilities. Alo and Lansky hit it off from the start. Both were small men, five foot three inches, and only a year apart in their ages. They were both basically shy men who had crawled out of the almost unbelievable poverty of the New York slums. They were book loving, low profile, chain-smokers without much to say to those they didn't know. Over the years, Alo had grown to represent Lansky's muscle, a perpetual reminder to the outside world that the reasonable and businesslike Lansky was protected by the Mafia.

They were alike on another level as well. Alo knew that Meyer wanted the same thing he did, a way out, respectability. Meyer had said once, "Don't worry, don't worry. Look at history. Look at the Astors and the Vanderbilt's, all those big society people. They were the worst thieves, and now look at them. It's just a matter of time." Before the end of the day, Jimmy Blue Eyes announced to Potatoes Kaufman that he had a new set of partners, and Kaufman, without any other avenues open to him, welcomed Alo with open arms.

When Meyer Lansky arrived in Hallendale to look over the casino he learned what Kaufman probably already knew, that the Plantation was about to be put out of business. A vigilante committee, concerned with the town's growth and public image, brought an injunction against the casino, called the Plantation, as a public nuisance and had secured a judgment against the property's land deed, which forbade gambling on the property. Lansky, always at his best in the worst situation, calmly examined the problem. He read the wording for the injunction carefully and saw that the judgment forbade gambling on a specific parcel of land, so Lansky decided to pick the casino up, place it on trucks and move it to a different parcel of land, end of problem. It was a brilliant move but still the nagging problem of concerned citizens had to be addressed, so Lansky placed his brother Jake, the casino's new manager, in charge of corrupting the town. Unlike Meyer or Alo, Jake had already made Hollywood his home, and within weeks of being given the job, Jake had doled out tens of thousands of dollars to the Elks, the Shiners, local hospitals.

With Lansky in control, the casino exceeded expectations and according to at least one gambling expert, the Barn may have been the biggest money-maker in the entire history of illegal casino gambling, bringing in an estimated $10 million a year between 1947 and 1949. With the profits they earned from the Plantation, Alo and Lansky opened another casino in Hallendale, the Colonial Inn, along with a small but lucrative handbook in Fort Lauderdale that they named "The It Club" and, old habits being hard to break, Alo and Bugsy Siegel, a childhood friend of Meyers, ran a bookie operation out of the Hollywood Yacht Club, if, for no other reason, they weren't supposed to do it.

By 1939, Siegel, who was then living between New York and Los Angeles, was a regular at Hallendale casinos in which he held a small interest. But it wasn't always in the casinos' best interest to have him around. Once, when a customer recognized him from his newspaper photographs, he walked over to Siegel's table and said, "Hello Bugsy!" Within seconds the customer was laying on the floor, his nose broken with Siegel standing over him, ranting, "Don't you ever call me Bugsy!" and then, before walking away, kicked the man in the ribs repeatedly. When Frank Costello, another owner in the casinos, heard what happened, he said, "You never should have kicked him in the ribs, that was bad manners." Business boomed, Meyer's friends opened a dog track in Hollywood in 1936 and three years later, other friends built the Gulf stream Race Track in Hallendale whose mile long entrance was lined with royal palms.

Where success goes, others follow and by 1948, Hallendale was "a gambler's paradise...a little Las Vegas before its time" and was sarcastically known as the "Wall Street of South Florida", due to its unusually high number of banks, investment and brokerage firms that cropped up in the area. More gamblers were opening bigger, better and cleaners casinos on the border of the Dade and Broward county lines, an estimated thirty-six carpet joints in all and then there were the smaller Mom and Pop backroom places, wire rooms, hundreds of crap game places, horse parlors run by snow bird Mafioso on vacation and wire rooms. And big name hoods like Bugsy Siegel, Moe Sedway, Joe Adonis and Longy Zwillman were Hallendale regulars making deep financial interests with Lansky and Jimmy Alo. The law wasn't a problem

Walter Clark was old time Broward county. Popular and likable with a pot belly, enormous hands and ready laugh, he had swept into office as Broward County Sheriff in a landslide vote in 1933, his campaign "funded" in no small part by Jimmy Alo. Once, when asked by a newsman why he allowed so much gambling to go on in Broward county, Sheriff Walter Clark answered: "Why? Because I'm a Goddamn liberal, that's why. I will not go around these parts and stick my nose into the private business of the people." When the governor's office asked why Clark didn't do anything about the gambling resorts that dotted the Broward-Dade lines, Clark said he had heard about those places, but as long as none of his constituents complained about them, so be it.

The Hallendale police force, three men in all, worked as traffic supervisors outside the casinos and the County sheriff would send over a squad of men each night to escort the casinos' manager to the banks nigh depository. The armored truck company that took the money from the bank was owned by Robert Clark, the sheriff's younger brother. Otherwise, justice in Hallendale in 1947 was swift and sure. There is the famous story of a hapless Black man, a field hand who had come into town and lost every cent he had in a crap game. To get money for food, he started to panhandle outside one of the casinos and was arrested on the spot by one of the town's three policemen. Brought before the court, presided over by H.L. Chancey, who was also the town's mayor, the man was found guilty and sentenced to one year at hard labor. The sentence was stayed in as long as the Black man agreed to leave town within ten minutes and never return again. Justice in Hallendale was also profitable. Under Judge Chancey's reign, the city made as much money from fines levied from bogus "disorderly conduct" charges as it did from standard taxes. Each Monday morning, the names of several representatives from the various casinos operating within the city limits appeared on Chancey's docket, charged with disorderly conduct. Chancey would impose a fine on each, the amount depending the gross receipts of the individual casinos they represented. The representatives were never actually in court, so a bailiff was sent to the casino managers with the bill for the fine.

"We filled up the treasury in the winter months," said Joe Varon who was then the city attorney, "and by the end of the summer we would be running low. So in September we would get a loan of ten thousand dollars from the bank to tide us over until the casinos opened again." By 1940, the "disorderly conduct" scam was a major source of income for the city and a large number of its citizens. Registered voters, there were only several hundred before the 1950s, received $35 over the course of the gambling season, about the size of the average middle class pay check back then. Hallandale's farmers also made a handsome living selling their products to the casinos' massive kitchens and the gambling dens provided well-paying employment for hundreds of locals, many of whom were recommended, in writing, by the city's mayor, H.C. Schwartz.

With the money they made from the Hallendale operations, Costello, Lansky and Alo founded the Emby Distributing Company, which had a lock on the distribution of jukeboxes and cigarette vending machines in the greater New York area. Working under a legitimate and exclusive license as the sole distributor on the East coast of the Wurlitzer Juke Box Corporation, Emby gave Lansky and his partners control of the popular music outlet during the 1940s and to no small degree Frank Sinatra's amazing career took off as a result of the hoods control of what records appeared in their jukeboxes. Unfortunately for Sinatra, Costello's mob was also pressing bootleg copies, millions of them, of Sinatra's records. Then the bosses at Wurlitzer realized who really ran Emby and asked Lansky, the group's front man, to sell out his routes. "They said I was a bad risk for them," Lansky said later, and without trouble, he and the others sold off their Juke Box routes to outside investors.

With the cash Lansky and Alo made from the sale of Embry (it's not known if Costello was involved), they invested in a corporation called Consolidated Television with $15,000, owning about 10% of the company. But the gangsters weren't able to understand the big picture behind television, they didn't understand how it could generate any steady cash, and that was the key word, cash, and in the late 1940s they withdrew from the business. When the war ended in 1945, Americans leaped into their search for relaxation and fun and for the first time, millions of them, loaded with cash, found it in Florida. So many people flooded into the Sunshine state, that for the first time, reservations were needed even in the smallest roadside motel, if one could be found.

Smack in the middle of all this post war wealth and affluence was the Lansky-Alo gambling operation which now included two more clubs, the Club Boheme on the coast road that offered gambling and a floor show and the Green Acres, which was off of Route US 1 which was still unlighted and unpaved. The Green Acres, which was actually little more than the packing plant it had been before Lansky converted it into a casino, offered old style gambling without chips, just dollar bills.

There was competition of course, mostly from independents operating down in Miami, that wasn't a problem. What was a problem for them was the ever-changing and complex politics of the area. Right after the war, Lee Hills, a bright and ambitious editor of the Miami Herald newspaper, launched a weekly series called "Know your neighbor" which not only identified known gamblers in the Miami area, it pasted their pictures alongside their home address. This prompted the mostly do-nothing Miami police to start raids on the casinos, and by early 1946, Lansky's competition from Miami was all but over.

Estes Kefauver took his committee to Florida and opened up an investigation into the campaign contributions to Governor Fuller Warren from mafia gambling syndicates made up of Chicago and New York organizations. Billy Johnston, who worked for Capone and later for Tony Accardo as Chicago's operative in Miami, was one of the governor's three largest contributors at just over $400,000. Johnson couldn't account for the source of the money and the fact that the contribution were uncovered at all made the bosses in Chicago very uneasy. In Broward county, County Sheriff Walter Clark was questioned for hours in public and all laid out his complicity in gambling there. All of the payoffs made by Lansky to the government and people of Hallendale were documented as business expenses by Lansky with IRS, since he feared a tax charge more than anything else, and Kefauver was using those records to close the city down. Kefauver's staff never actually went to Hallendale, but described it as "the sin city capitol of the South, a wide open den of inequity." But although the committee never went to Hallendale, after those statements television stations from around the world flooded into the city reporting on everything. But, aside from the closed casinos, they found very little in the way of sin. In fact, Broward county was one of the safest, crime free areas in the world.

Unlike Miami, which the Chicago and Trafficante mobs had flooded with prostitutes and underground porn shops, Broward had few if any hookers in operation largely because they were bad for the gambling business. Anything that took the men away from the tables to spend their money elsewhere, was bad for business. Lansky appeared before the committee three times, all to undramatic results, except one. During questioning by Kefauver, Lansky asked, "What's wrong with gambling, Senator? I mean you like it yourself. I know you've gambled a lot."

"That's true," Kefauver responded, "that's quite right, I do," referring to his large, but legal, bets at racetracks. "But I don't want you people to control it."

Lansky, assuming that Kefauver meant Jews and Italians instead of gangsters fired back, "I'm not one of those Jewish hotel owners in Miami Beach who tell you all sorts of stories just to please you," referring to the parade of hotel investors who appeared before the committee testifying about gambling in Florida. "I will not allow you to persecute me because I am a Jew." Kefauver's response was to have a federal grand jury return a 21 count indictment against Lansky for his dealing in corrupting racetrack gambling. He pled guilty to five counts and was given three months and a fine of $2,500 plus probation. It was a slap on the wrist and the underworld figured that he had fixed the courts, but he didn't. At best the indictment was weak but it served its purpose, it punished Lansky. Still, as a result of Kefauver's attention, there was a general assault of federal and Florida State inspectors into the Broward county. The massive Boheme and Green Acres casinos were closed and Lansky, Alo and others were arrested and convicted on gambling charges there as well. That charge, a felony, stripped Lansky of his civil right to vote which the government had managed to hold in suspension until 1974. When the government finally dropped its claim, Joe Varon, using his considerable contacts in the Florida State capitol, had the conviction dropped, telling the Governor's office that the conviction was a technicality, it was thirty years old and reflected the values of a different age. So at age 83, Lansky could now vote.

The attention that Kefauver brought closed down Hallendale as an open city. Hallendale was closing anyway, and it had been since 1947, when Hollywood moved to shut down gambling within its city limits and the state of Florida started to snoop around the area, thanks largely to the efforts of R.H. Gore, publisher of the local newspaper, whom Lansky tried to bribe. The Hollywood problem started in 1947, when a local lawyer named William Flacks took the floor during a town meeting and asked the mayor, Robert Haymaker, what he intended to do about gambling. "You know the situation," the lawyer said, "and you know that the police chief has been given no instruction to stop it. You know that every tavern, every pool room and nightspot runs gambling. It's got to come to a stop and I ask for a motion from the floor to stop it." Mayor Haymaker was quick on his feet. "Every citizen," he said, "should proceed on his own account." But Flacks wouldn't back down and before the meeting ended, the Hollywood police chief was instructed to shut down gambling, every type and sort, in Hollywood city limits. A few months later, citizens of Hallendale, inspired by its neighbors' clean up, started rumbling about closing down the casinos there and in February of 1948, the Colonial Inn was closed.

In 1948, Lansky sold one of his Hallendale casinos to New York burlesque impresario John Minsky, leaving a heavy hint that he intended to sell all of his casinos to Minsky, leaving the Hallendale vigilantes to decide if they wanted illegal gambling in their city or legal strip clubs. They took the clubs. In 1949, Lansky was allowed to reopen his casinos. But the signals had been sent. The end was near, postwar prosperity to the county meant they no longer needed the money casinos could bring in. The image of lawlessness that came with casinos was bad for the county's image. It was time to move along. Vegas was a possibility. In 1948, Meyer funded the Thunderbird casino and placed his brother Jake inside the counting room to make sure no one stole money from the money they were stealing. But Vegas was dominated by the Chicago outfit and it was still, in 1948 with only four casinos, little more than the desert strip Bugsy Siegel had found it to be ten years before. Instead, Lansky turned his attention to Cuba. But Cuba turned out to be a bust and the partners finally looked to Las Vegas.

A year after the Sands casino opened its doors in Las Vegas in 1951, Jack Dragna, the head of the Los Angeles mob, the so-called Micky Mouse Mafia, moved in on Sedway, who was known to be Meyer Lansky's representative at the Flamingo . Apparently, Dragna had cleared the assault with Thomas "Tommy Brown" Lucchese in New York although it's more likely that Dragna, who worked directly under Chicago's control, actually gave the okay to appease the powerful Tony Accardo who had decided back in 1947 that he wanted his family to run Vegas. Dragna sent one of his men, Jimmy "The Weasel" Fratianno, who would later turn mob informant, to send a message to Moe Sedway, Meyer Lansky's five foot, 130-pound front man in Vegas who had started as a gofer for Lansky back in New York. Fratianno caught up with him as he left the lobby of the Wilshire Hotel in Los Angeles and was trying to flag a cab. Fratianno grabbed Sedway from behind and swung him around by the neck. "Moey, I want to tell you something, you motherfucker. You better walk straight around Vegas because the next time I'm going to blow your fucking head off." Then he backhanded Sedway across the mouth, drawing blood.

The Flamingo Hotel Casino under construction

"What's the matter with you?" Sedway cried. "Leave me alone."

"Remember, you better walk straight." It was a Sicilian message that Sedway and Lansky understood. They had been moved on. Five days later Doc Starcher, Lansky's other front man in Vegas also got a visit from Jimmy the Weasel. Starcher had a record for assault and battery, robbery, burglary, bootlegging and hijacking and suspicion of murder. He had been under Longy Zwillman in New Jersey and for a while was a power in Newark politics. Then Lansky had picked him to oversee the building of the Sands in Vegas. Fratianno caught him between two sets of glass doors at the entrance to the Sands. "Listen you motherfucker. I want to tell you something. You're around here high rolling like a fucking big shot, you better do the right thing," and then backhanded him across the mouth, drawing blood. "You better walk straight in this town, or I'll blow your fucking head off," and then Fratianno worked him over. Starcher was small but he was tough but still there was nothing he could do, Fratianno was a made member of the Mafia, if he touched him, even to defend himself, he was a dead man.

GRAND OPENING
of Las Vegas' newest
$5,000000 Resort
Thursday and Friday, Dec. 26-27
Flamingo

Lansky went to Lucchese. "What's the matter with that fucking weasel? What's his problem? First he whacks Moey Sedway and then he whacks Doc Starcher. He told them to walk straight or he'll blow their heads off. Listen Tommy, these guys are in my fucking family. Who does this weasel think he is anyway?" Lucchese said, "Well, you know, he's their top man out there. He's done a lot of work for LA and they're fucking starving out there."

The Flamingo 1946

Lansky said, "So they're putting the arm on us, is that what this is?"

"Listen Meyer, that's their country you're in, don't forget that."

Lansky yelled, "That's open country out there! They got no right to smack my people!" Lucchese remained calm and said, "What? You want to start a fucking war? They've got to make a living. What do they care about open country? Vegas is in their back yard." It took a year to work out but in early 1954 Lansky sent word to Dragna that he could buy into the Flamingo for $125,000 but Dragna declined.

In 1952, Jimmy Alo started flying out to Las Vegas on a regular basis to oversee construction of his latest investment, the Sands Casino, which opened in the first part of the year. Jimmy had to go because Meyer Lansky, his partner in the project, was under constant surveillance by one law enforcement arm or another, and would bring down too much heat if he toured the famous Strip that he virtually built and owned. Meyer had chosen "Doc" Stacher to run the place with Babe Baron who looked after the Chicago mob's interests.

Tommy Lucchese

The others owners in the Sands included Joe Fusco, Longy Zwillman, Tony Accardo, Sam Giancana, and the Chicago outfit, as well as Abe Teitelbaum, a dark mob figure who had once been one of Al Capone's many lawyers. Gerardo Catena, a boss out in New Jersey owned another piece and so did Frank Sinatra. It was generally agreed by most organized crime experts that Sinatra was probably fronting ownership for the Chicago outfit's leadership. But Sinatra wouldn't come into the deal, officially anyway, until 1954, the year he won his Academy Award for his role in the film, From Here to Eternity. Sinatra and Jimmy Blue Eyes went way back, in fact in 1952, Jimmy Blue Eyes became part of Hollywood legend when Frank Sinatra, at a low point in his career, needed a role in a war film to bring life back to his sagging career. Then, in 1954, after he won his Academy Award and construction on the Sands was completed, Sinatra applied for a casino gambling license from the state of Nevada. It was big news in Hollywood where it was widely rumored that the crooner was dead broke. A hearing was held in Reno and it was learned that Sinatra had already bought 2% of the Sands with $54,000, which one of the hearing administrators objected to since he felt that the singer should have used the money to pay off the $109,000 federal tax bill that he owed. A Justice department investigation would later show that one stockholder in the casino was persuaded to sell Sinatra two of his five shares for $70,000 and that the additional 7 points that the singer later owned in the hotel were given to him by Jimmy Blue Eyes as a gift.

Jimmy Blue Eyes would spend most of the last half of 1952 and early 1953 in Las Vegas, settling one dispute after another, including the Dragna problem. By 1960, The Sands had become the very definition of a mobbed up casino so it was almost fitting that it became the place where Frank Sinatra introduced Presidential candidate John Kennedy to Judy Campbell, a women with no recognizable employment who would eventually "date," as she called it, Chicago mob boss Sam Giancana and his West Coast lackey, Johnny Roselli. This was how Campbell came to be invited to watch Sinatra and his Rat Pack perform at the Sands Casino in Vegas on February 7, 1960. During the performance, Kennedy sat with Judy Campbell, who said that she had no idea who the Presidential candidate was, and that they got along so well that after the show, Campbell joined Kennedy at his press conference in the casino lobby, and later had lunch with him in Sinatra's hotel suite.

The FBI already had the place under surveillance in early 1960 and noted that "It is a known fact that the Sands Hotel is owned by Hoodlums and while the Senator (Kennedy), Sinatra and (Peter) Lawford were there, show girls from all over the town were running in and out of the Senator's suite." "Show girls" was a euphemism for the high dollar prostitutes that worked the casino on a regular basis and were paid by the house to service the rooms. During that particular party, Kennedy's brother-in-law Peter Lawford took singer Sammy Davis aside and whispered, "If you want to see what a million in cash looks like, go into the next room. There's a brown leather satchel in the closet filled with a million. It's a gift from the hotel owners to Jack."

On one trip out to Vegas, Jimmy Alo was greeted at the airport by Jack Entratter, the onetime doorman-bouncer at the Stork Club in Manhattan before moving over to the Copacabana before Alo offered him a job out in Vegas overlooking the Sands Casino with a 12 point interest in the place, or at least on the books. It was Entratter who Sinatra had called after Harry Cohn turned him down for the role of Maggio. Entratter was a close, personal friend of Harry Cohn, they were regular fishing partners on weekends, but even the phone calls from Entratter didn't budge Cohn to hand the part to Sinatra. Then, according to Johnny Roselli, Entratter went directly to Frank Costello on Sinatra's behalf. In reality, Entratter only owned two points in the Sands, the other ten points were held by him, in his name for persons who preferred to remain in the shadows or like Alo, had criminal records and ownership in the casino might endanger the casino license.

Jimmy Alo. Early in his criminal career in New York he was dubbed Jimmy Blue Eyes for his ability to deal with Irish criminals and politicians (Who were called "The Blue Eyes" by the old Mustache Petes who then ruled the Underworld)

Nor was Entratter actually the Sands manager, everyone knew that Doc Stacher was the real power at the casino, meaning that Entratter's only real use at the Sands was to ensure that the hidden owners got their money out of the place. Once at the Sands, Entratter took Alo up to his new suite, which he had built for himself to his own specifications at a cost of one million dollars. With a huge cigar rammed into his fat face, Entratter, followed by a swarm of casino executives, gloated over every detail of the apartment to Alo. Alo was already out of sorts by what was going on at the casino with Sinatra, who was, by now, an executive Vice President in the Sands Corporation and pulling down $100,000 a week when he performed there, and Frank performed there a lot.

Sinatra had a three-bedroom suit on the ground floor, he was afraid of heights, a private swimming pool to go along with his private sauna and steam bath. The casino footed the bill when Frank had specialty meats flown in from Manhattan, and the boys looked the other way when Sinatra cursed and screamed at the hire help because the color of the phone in his room was blue instead of orange. The boys had given Frank $3,000 a night to gamble with at the casino, but he often went through that in less than a half hour, drew a marker and never paid it back. Alo grew more and more angry at the vulgar display and finally he exploded. "You son of a bitch! I should'a left you as a head waiter! You come over here and spend millions of dollars. You smoke big cigars. You dress in two thousand dollars suits. And you're nothing more than a lackey. I should send you all back where you belong!"

Alo had enough, enough of Vegas, enough of Sinatra, enough of the new brand of slick-backed, ego-ridden hoods who couldn't keep their faces off the front page or the nightly news.   It was time to cash in their chips. "Let's take the money," Jimmy Blue Eyes told Meyer Lansky, "and have a quiet life."

In 1967, Lansky and Alo realized a profit of just over $1 million dollars each when their man Jack Entratter, working under the guidance of Moe Dalitz, dumped the Sands Casino to Howard Hughes for $14.6 million. No one will ever know how much they made off the sale of their Vegas holdings. But as Chicago front man in Vegas told his Los Angeles counterpart, Jimmy the Weasel Fratianno, "Meyer Lansky and his group have skimmed more money than anybody in the world. Just in Vegas alone over the past ten years from the Flamingo, the Sands, the Thunderbird, the Riviera, they skimmed three hundred million easy. And that's not counting the millions taken from joints in New York, Florida, Kentucky, Louisiana, and Arkansas. Or all those years in Cuba, and now the Bahamas and England." Replacing the Italian gangsters and their Jewish front men were well-heeled entrepreneurs with Ivy League MBA's who reinvented and restructured the Vegas built by hoods with names like Bugsy and Tony the Hat. Under the watch of these blue suited wonder kids, Vegas became a corporate town and that's when the real money was made, tens of millions of dollars were gained from the value of prime Las Vegas real estate and the new luxury mega hotels that were slapped up on the Strip over the next decade, funded in large part by the junk bond, merger and acquisition frenzy of the 1980's.
(See also Moey Sedway)

*****

Sedway Morris: Casino operator. Born Sedwits and legally changed to Sedway in 1924. AKA Moey. AKA Moe. Born 1894. Died 1952. Born in Poland. Arrived in the United States in 1921. Became a US citizen on July 16, 1914. Lived at 614 North Beverly Drive in Beverly Hill, California. Sedway was essentially a gofer, a hanger-on for Meyer Lansky and later for Bugsy Siegel, and for the most part was not affiliated with the muscle end of the rackets business. He did have a criminal past. He was arrested in 1917 for grand larceny and in 1919 for unlawful entry. "It was on a Saturday afternoon" Sedway recalled "and we were running a crap game in the loft up in the twenties. I don't remember what street it was. And it was raided, and I was arrested with one other man, charged with unlawful entry....I went to the reformatory for 3 months to 3 years. I did a little less than a year. I was 22 years old, I think."

He was arrested for assault and robbery in 1928 "But I was arrested in an office on Broadway, and they charged me with assault and robbery of a person and the person was called in and failed to identify, and I was released. That is one of those things. You are Mr. Halley, aren't you ? In order to hold you in New York City, they fix—they put a charge on you regardless of what it is, to keep you overnight, to bring you into court." On July 6 1931, he was arrested for his role in stealing $200,000 in treasury notes but was acquitted in the case. He was named as the go-between in the 1936, $20,000 extortion of the Gottfried Baking Company to settle a labor dispute. His last arrest came in 1940 in San Diego for gambling and arrested in Albany New York for vagrancy (A reduced charge from gambling) His own steady job, outside of gambling, was running a trucking business with his brother-in-law and a Chinese restaurant, Fu Manchu, in New York for a few years. Sedway followed Siegel to Las Vegas in 1938. "I came here" he told the Kefauver Committee "and I had a part interest in the Northern Club book. I came here at the request of Ben Siegel. He had bought in with Dave Stearns in the Northern Club and lie asked me to come down here, and he gave me a piece of the book to look out for his interests. Although he had begun traveling to Las Vegas in the very early 1920s to build up gambling interest in Nevada and California. Sedway was also a crucial link in developing the mob wire service, Trans-America Race Wire Service. In 1945, Sedway and Gus Greenbaum were the owner on record of the El Cortez Hotel in Vegas and posted record profits. In 1950, while he was, on record anyway, part owner of the Flamingo casino in Las Vegas he was called before the Kefauver Committee to answer questions about the Outfits holdings in Nevada. He testified that he was ill "I have had three major coronary thrombosis, and I have had diarrhea for 6 weeks, and I have an ulcer, hemorrhoids, and an abscess on my upper intestines. I just got out of bed and I am loaded with drugs." Sedway, who was the head of the Las Vegas United Jewish Appeal, died of a heart attack, shortly before midnight on January 4, 1952, while on vacation in Florida. Three hundred people attended his funeral. His honorary pallbearers included Dean Martin, The Marx Brothers, Jerry Lewis, The Ritz Brother, Spike Jones, Eddie Canton and Danny Thomas.
(See also The Greenbaum murder case)

*****

Schachter, Harry: AKA Harry Greenberg. A childhood friend of Bugsy Siegel who later worked for Lucky Luciano and Meyer Lansky. On November 22, 1939, Siegel and his brother-in-law, Whitey Krakower, murdered Schachter outside of his home, in an ambush, at 1804 Vista Del Mar Drive. Other suspected in the killing were Frankie Carbo (Who was later accused of murdering Siegel) and Al Tannenbaum

*****

Siegel Bugsy: Born in Brooklyn as Benjamin Hyman Siegel. One of five children of Austrian-Jewish immigrant parents. Siegel spoke German. Casino owner. Born February 28, 1906. Died June 20, 1947. When the Gangster Chronicles came on television in the late 1970's, a relative of Bugsy Siegel remarked to Meyer Lansky, Siegel's lifelong business partner, that he was considering suing the production company for depicting Bugsy as an uncontrollable killer.

Siegel

"What are you going to sue them for?" asked Lansky. "In real life he was worse."

Unlike most hoods who dominated gangdom in the 1930's, Siegel was smart and he knew it. He hated the poverty and ignorance of the world he was raised in and detested the illiterate and uncouth men he had to deal with. He wanted more, he wanted to be on the other side. In fact, Siegel wanted to be on the other side, the legitimate side, so badly, that he invested a million dollars in the stock market in 1933, but lost half of it when the market crashed in October. "If I had kept that million," he said, "I'd have been out of the rackets right now."

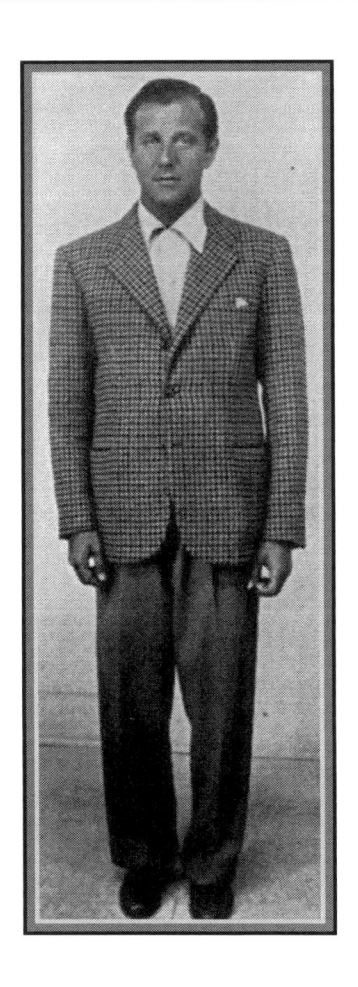

Siegel knew that if he stayed in New York, nothing would ever change, so he, and not the New York branch of the syndicate as is commonly reported, decided to try his luck out west in Los Angeles. He had been a regular visitor out there since 1933, introducing himself as an independent sportsman, a title that didn't fool anybody.

Of course, Bugsy had other motives. Gangsters always do. He had stabbed another hood in a dispute over a card game, cutting the man in the stomach 20 times to make sure gases would not allow his body to float to the surface, and now the cops wanted to talk to him about that. He had also been named in a scam to fix boxing matches and had ordered the killing of a bookie who had cheated him. When the bookie found out about the death order, he went to the cops and told them everything he knew, so for the time being it was best he went to the West Coast.

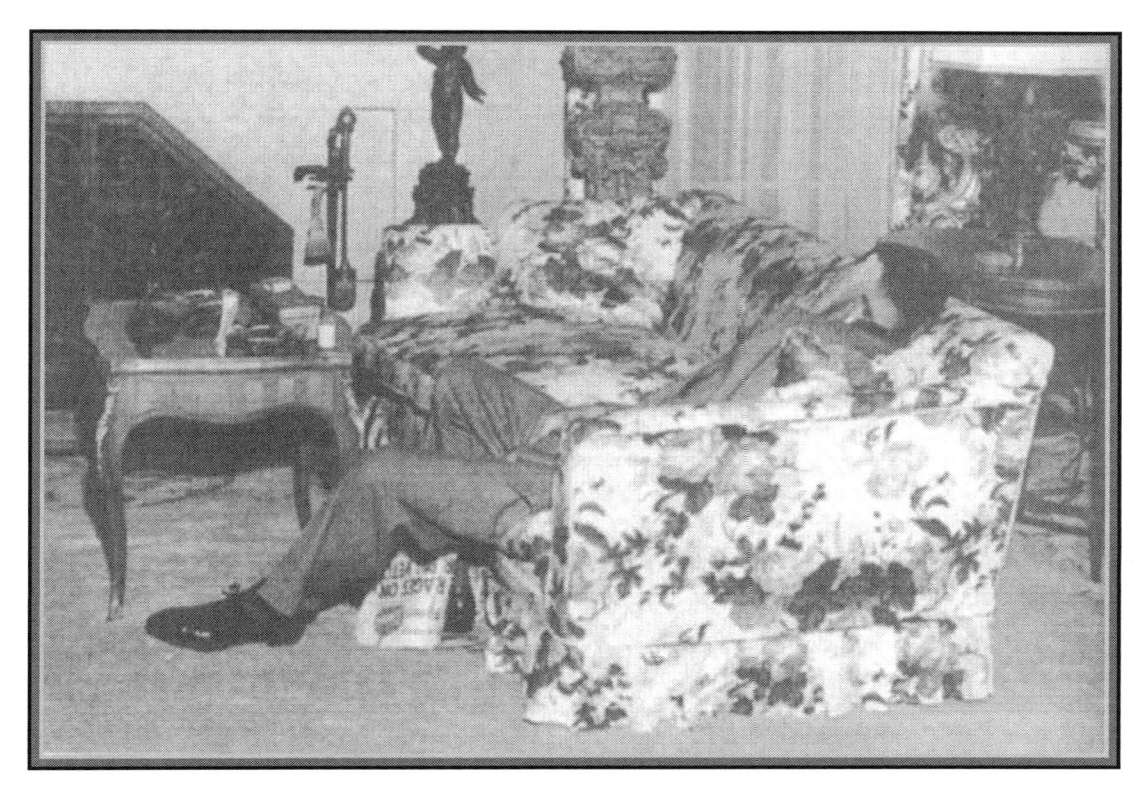

Siegel dead

Siegel took over the Screen Extras Guild and the Los Angeles Teamsters, which he ran until his death. With control of the Screen Extras Guild, Siegel was able to shake down Warner Brothers Studios for $10,000, with a refusal to provide extras for any of their films. He also shook down his movie star friends for huge loans that he never paid back, and when he came back for another loan, he always got it, because they were, justifiably, terrified of him.

He once bragged to Lansky that he had fleeced the Hollywood crowd out of more than $400,000 within six months of his arrival. He was a one man terrorist campaign.

When Siegel arrived in LA, the number one racing service out west was James Ragen's Continental Press, which serviced thousands of bookies between Chicago to Los Angeles, each of whom paid Ragen between $100 to $1200. The owner, Jimmy Ragen, was a tough, two fisted, Chicago born Irishman, who had punched, stabbed, and shot his way to the top of the heap, without the Mob's help.

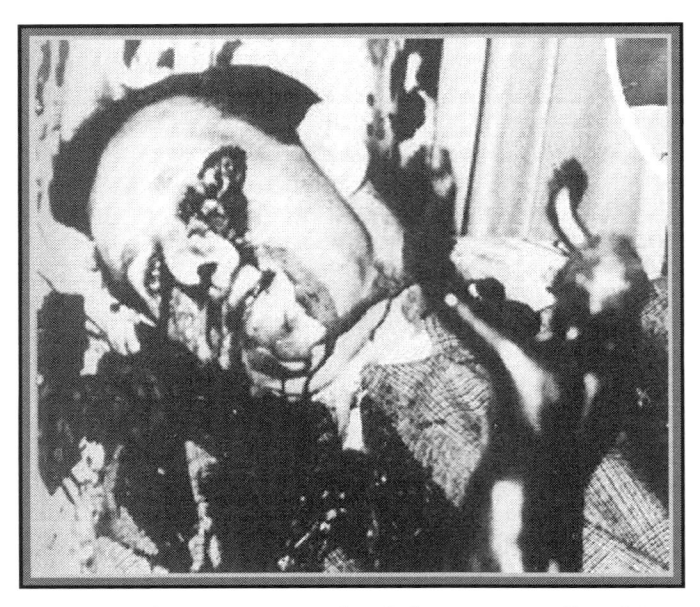

The Chicago outfit, then under Nitti, watched the money flood into Regan's office with envy. Nitti, and later Paul Ricca, tried to set up a rival service called Trans-American, with each mob boss across the country running the local outlet, doing whatever they had to do to take Ragen out of business.

In California, Siegel and Mafiosi Jack Dragna were charged with putting Trans-America in business and taking Ragen's Continental Press out of business. Eventually, the Chicago mob settled the entire issue by shooting Ragen as he drove his car down a Chicago street. Ragen survived the shooting, but not the dose of mercury a nurse working for the outfit shot up into his vein a few days later. With Ragen dead, Continental Racing Services was divided up among the various bosses who had helped to build it, and Jack Dragna was named to run the California office. Siegel was shocked. He had risked his life to build the service out west, he had worked on it day and night, at the least he expected to be cut in on perhaps half the franchise.

Instead, all he was got was a visit from Chicago's chief fixer, Murray Humphreys, who told Siegel to fold up Trans-America wire service. They didn't need it anymore. The syndicate owned Continental Press. But Siegel sent Humphreys packing with a message for Paul Ricca... if the Chicago people wanted Siegel to fold up Trans-America in Nevada, Arizona and Southern California, it would cost them $2,000,000 in cash.

Even though the Chicago outfit didn't want Siegel working for them, at the same time, they didn't want him working for New York either. Crazy or not, Siegel was smart, ambitious and ruthless. They had to watch him, so Paul Ricca told Charlie Fischetti, one of his most dependable torpedoes, to send out a spy, and the woman they chose was the same woman Bugsy Siegel came to call his Flamingo, Virginia Hill.

The Flamingo Casino, early 1950s

Virginia Hill was a foul-mouthed, tough-talking product of the poverty of Bessemer, Alabama who came to Chicago when she was 17, to find work in the Century of Progress Exhibition of 1933. She worked at a variety of jobs across the city, including a stint as a shimmy dancer for $20 a week, but, finally ended up as a street hooker, turning tricks for as little as fifty cents or as much as five dollars, it depended on how desperate the John was.

Virginia eventually fell under the command of Charlie and Joe Fischetti, who were heading up the mob's prostitution rackets at the time. Virginia was, more or less, adopted by Jake Guzik and his wife, who offered to put her in charge of several brothels they still owned, but Virginia turned them down. She said she had higher aspirations. But what she did take from Guzik was an introduction to Joe Epstein, or Joey Epp, as he liked to be called, a mild-mannered, middle class, mob accountant who wore thick black glasses and barely spoke to those around him. Nevertheless, he was dependable and honest, by mob standards, and had been Guzik's understudy since 1930 and would one day be his second-in-command.

Epp ran the outfit's racetracks with such authority the newspapers called him Illinois' unofficial racetrack commissioner. And while Epstein was well read, some said an intellectual, he loved to party and he was fascinated by the lowlife around him. He fell head over heels in love with Virginia Hill, and put her on the payroll as his mistress.

But it was a working relationship as well. Epstein put Virginia to work as a courier, bringing suitcases full of the mob's dirty money from Chicago, Kansas City, Cleveland and Los Angeles to syndicate owned and run banks in Cuba, Mexico, the Dominican Republic, France and Switzerland. There, the money was laundered, usually at a price of ten cents on a dollar and then invested in legitimate business from which the hoods could draw a salary.

The second part of the plan called for Virginia to get in touch with Bugsy Siegel, which she did, having met, and romanced him, several times in the past. Like Joey Epp before him, Bugsy Siegel fell head over heels in love with Virginia. He called her his "Flamingo" and drenched her in jewelry, furs and gowns.

Bugsy Siegel

Virginia reported every conversation she had with Siegel back to the Fischetti brothers in Chicago. Still, the boys back in Chicago never trusted Hill, or anyone else for that matter, and when Paul Ricca came to power, he told Johnny Roselli (1033 Wilshire Blvd. Los Angeles) to start an affair with Hill so he could keep tabs on her.

Then, Siegel watched a colorful Los Angeles hood named Tony Cornero move his entire gambling organization out of California and into Nevada where he and his brothers opened a rundown but very profitable casino on the Vegas Strip. Within a year, Siegel had the cash, most of it from the New York end of the syndicate, to build the fabulous Flamingo Hotel.

In May of 1947, one month before he was executed, Bugsy Siegel called Jimmy Fratianno, a Los Angeles hood who, technically anyway, worked for Chicago, and asked him to come out to Las Vegas for a meeting. He didn't tell them what it concerned, but, as they found out, it was a recruitment drive. He had already made the same pitch to Jack Dragna, Bugsy Siegel was planning the unheard of, he was going to start his own organization out in the Nevada desert.

Virginia Hill had already reported Siegel's plans to Paul Ricca in Chicago, and, even though the Chicago mob was chiseling Siegel in the Flamingo by sending in professional gamblers to break the bank, they were indignant. As far as they were concerned, although the syndicate had agreed to allow Vegas and Reno to operate as open cities, it was clearly understood in the syndicate that Chicago controlled everything west of the Mississippi.

Siegel was a regional problem at a time when the mob thought it had gotten over its regional misunderstandings. He was a relic from the past. He had to be removed.

On June 8, 1947, Virginia Hill got a call from Epstein back in Chicago, he told her to get out of town, to go to France, she could tell Siegel she was going there to buy wine for the casino as she had in the past. He wouldn't question that. Virginia knew, immediately, why she had to leave town. They were going to kill Bugsy and the boys back in Chicago didn't want their best cash courier and narcotics peddler splattered with blood and headlines. Virginia flew into Chicago and met Epstein at Midway airport, where he gave her $5,000 and then she continued to Paris.

Back on the West Coast, Bugsy Siegel, caught in the middle of an uprising, was too busy to care where Virginia was. Several days before, Siegel told Micky Cohen to tell all of the bookies in Los Angeles, Reno and Vegas that the price for using the wire service was going to double. But, to Siegel's amazement, the bookies refused to pay, they knew that Chicago was taking over and that they were planning to kill Siegel.

And, on June 20, 1947, that's what they did.

Jack Dragna gave the order to a hood named Frankie Carranzo. When the call came, Carranzo drove up to Beverly Hills and parked his car a few feet from Siegel's home, wound the silencer onto the barrel of his .30 caliber, army issue carbine, and walked around to the back of the house. He hid in the shadow of a rose-covered lattice work with his army carbine and released an entire clip into the living room through a 14-inch pane of glass.

Nine slugs in all. Two of them tore apart Bugsy's face as he sat on a chintz-covered couch. One bullet smashed the bridge of his nose and drove into his left eye. The eye was later found on the dining room floor, fifteen feet away from his dead body. The bullet was found in an English painting on the wall. The other entered his right cheek, passed through the back of his neck, and shattered a vertebra, ripped across the room.

At exactly 11:00 A.M., Jack Dragna got a call from Carranzo: "The insect was killed," and he then hung up.

A few minutes before that call, at 10:55, Little Moe Sedway and Gus Greenbaum, two hoods with gambling backgrounds, strode into the Flamingo and announced over the intercom system, "OK, we're taking over."

Everyone present knew who "we" were.

The only persons to attend Siegel's funeral services at Beth Olam Cemetery were his brother and a Rabbi.

Virginia Hill continued working for the Chicago outfit as a courier for several more years before they replaced her in 1950. She married a guy who wasn't involved with the outfit and had a child, but that ended in divorce.

Joey Epp never fell out of love with her, and he kept her on the books for as long as they bosses would let him, but eventually even that stopped.

When it did, it was widely rumored in gangland that Virginia, desperate for cash, started to extort money out of Joe Adonis and other mob guys for whom she had carried narcotics over the years. On March 24, 1966, near a brook in Koppl Austria, a small town near Salzburg, two hikers found Virginia Hill's dead body. Austrian officials, not understanding who Hill had been, ruled her unusual death a suicide by poison.

The Flamingo's next manager was Gus Greenbaum. He did his job. The hotel was completed and enlarged from 97 to two hundred rooms. By the end of the year the casino posted a $4 million profit, $15 million before the skim, clearing the way for the skimming to begin

*****

Shenker, Morris: Casino operator. Died August 10, 1989 at age 82. A Russian born Jew, who had survived, even prospered in the Las Vegas underworld. He arrived in St. Louis in 1922, at age 15, able to speak only a few words of English. Shenker worked his way through law school at Washington University and went into practice in 1932. He was one the world's leading fundraisers for Israel. Called the "foremost lawyer for the mob in the U.S.," by Life Magazine, Shenker was a defense attorney from St. Louis who represented Teamsters' President James R. Hoffa.   Although he represented leading Mafia killers in St. Louis, Shenker was active in Democratic politics and was appointed by St. Louis Mayor A. J. Cervantes to serve as chair of the St. Louis Commission on Crime and Law Enforcement. Shenker was forced to resign amid allegations that money from a $20 million dollar federal grant to fight crime was going to "unauthorized persons and causes "on the commission.

In 1983, federal agents investigating the skim at the Dunes Hotel in Las Vegas, owned largely by Shenker, (The secret owner, or least the major stockholder, of the Dunes was said to be Ray Patriarca, boss of the Rhode Island Mafia) discovered a multimillion-dollar fraud perpetuated by Russian-American gangster Evsei Agron, Murray Wilson and allegedly by Shenker. According to the Justice Department, Shenker had arranged for Agron and a dozen members of his crew to fly into Las Vegas on all-expense-paid junkets. He then insured that each of the hoods with Agron were given lines of credit of up to $50,000. However, instead of gambling the money, they turned the chips over to Wilson who cashed them in and Shenker never repaid the casino for the markers. Over a period of several months, the scam defrauded the Dunes of more than $1 million. The government believed that Shenker had masterminded the scheme. Shenker eventually managed to drive the once proud Dunes Casino into Chapter 11. Indicted for personal bankruptcy fraud in 1989, he died before the government could prosecute him.

*****

Spilotro Anthony: Tony Spilotro got into the mob largely because his father ran an old style Italian restaurant frequented by Paul Ricca and the older, powerful mob bosses. Ricca and the others took young Spilotro under their wings and corrupted him. While he was barely out of his teens, the ambitious Spilotro was hand-picked by Sam Giancana to become an enforcer for his old friend "Mad Sam" DeStefano, an insane killer and juice lender.

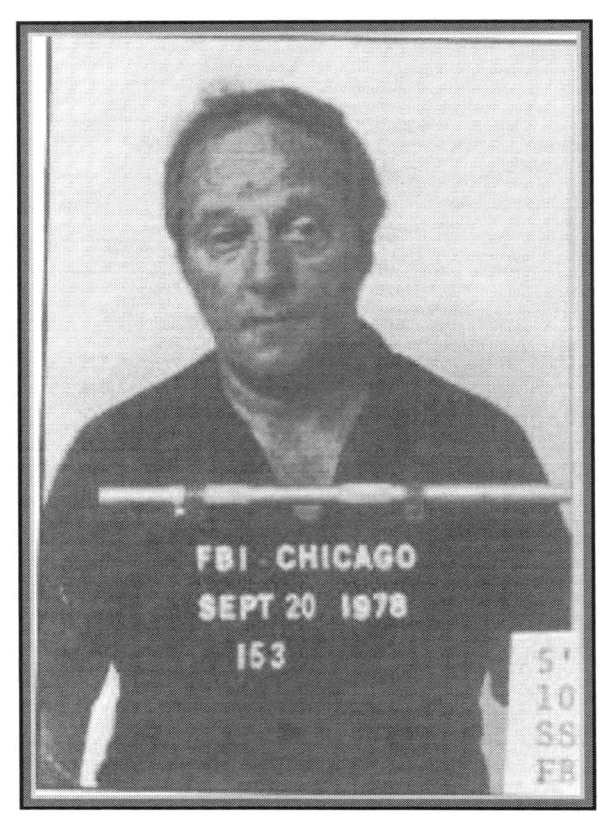

Victor Spilotro, Tony Spilotro Brother

In the late 1960s, just after he shot gunned his boss Mad Sam to death, on orders from above, the bosses sent Tony out west to Vegas as their representative to the casinos. In effect he was the most powerful hood in the country, west of Chicago. But, where the past, Vegas Enforcers only killed when ordered, Spilotro seemed to solve every problem by murder. The FBI suspected Tony of no less than 25 murders while he was Chicago's man in Vegas. Then, in the early 1980s, five men from Tony's crew became government witnesses and testified against big shots back home like Aiuppa and Cerone. Spilotro himself was indicted in Nevada for heading a burglary ring within Las Vegas city limits, a serious violation of mob rules and for having an affair with the outfit's man inside the Stardust, Frank "Lefty" Rosenthal.

At first, the bosses figured they would punish Spilotro with a demotion. Then he tried to blow Rosenthal up, in the middle of Vegas and there were rumors that the Ant was doing too much cocaine and was thinking about flipping over to the FBI. Tony and his brother, Michael, were last seen the afternoon of June 14, 1986, when they left Michael Spilotro's Oak Park home to run an errand. It is believed that Sam "Wings" Carlisi, ordered Michael, or Micky as he was called, to bring his brother out to the Indian cornfield where they were both killed. Several days after they left home, the partially clad bodies of the two brothers were unearthed from a five-foot grave in a cornfield a hundred yards off the main road near Morocco, Indiana. They had been beaten, kicked, stomped and presumably buried alive by their assailants. While it is commonly assumed that Micky Spilotro was in the wrong place at the wrong time, the fact is, that he had been in training under his brother, who was grooming him to take his place in Vegas as the Outside man.

Michael Spilotro (AKA Micky Born September 12, 1944 Died 1986) on the record anyway, was the manager of Hoagie's Pub on the west side. He entered the mob in about 1980. A friend of actor Robert Conrad, Spilotro appeared as a stick-up man in Conrad's TV series The Duke in 1979. He later was featured in Will: The Autobiography of G. Gordon Liddy as well as with Tom Selleck in Magnum P.I. in the "Thicker than Blood" episode. By the mid-1980s, Spilotro was involved in bookmaking, drug dealing, prostitution, robbery and extortion. He was murdered, along with his brother Tony June 14, 1986.

The third Spilotro brother, Victor (Spilotro Victor P: Lived at 2152 North Melvina Avenue in Chicago. Born 1935.) was the eldest Spilotro. It was not until the 1980s, that Victor started to get public attention. In 1980, Victor was convicted of gambling and tax fraud charges in connection with an illegal bookmaking operation disguised as a racetrack messenger service. Victor was sentenced to 18 months and was out in 13 months.

In 1986, Victor's brothers, Tony and Michael, were found dead in a Indiana cornfield. A year later, he was recognized as a member of the Chicago Outfit. In 1987 he was tried on fraud and extortion charges, accused of accepting $40,000 in protection money between 1981 and 1984 from the National Credit Card Service, an illegal credit card company that processed payments made to prostitutes. The firm actually was set up by the Federal Bureau of Investigation in a probe of vice in suburban Chicago. Spilotro, fifty-two, was found Guilty but received a light penalty from a judge who commented, "It is a troublesome case. If your name wasn't Spilotro, you wouldn't be here." On July 17, 1987, Victor was sentenced to six months of work release and five years' probation. He died in January of 1997 in a Wheeling health-care facility. Of the remaining brothers Pasquale Spilotro became an oral surgeon and dentist in the Chicago and Vincent more or less lived a law-abiding life. John Victor and Michael were professional criminals.

*****

Stacher Joseph: Gambler. AKA Doc Born 1902 Died 1977 Born under the last name Oystacher in the Ukraine. Starcher arrived in the United States with his family in 1912 when he was ten years old. By the early 1920s, he was selling beer to distributors for Abner "Longy" Zwillman, in New Jersey. He was eventually promoted to manage Zwillman's extensive gambling operations in Northern New Jersey. In the 1930s, Stacher was working for Meyer Lansky in the West Coast and the Caribbean. When Las Vegas began to grow, Lansky moved Stacher to Nevada to oversee his interests there at the Sands and later at the Freemont Casinos. In the early 1960s, Stacher fell into Attorney General Bobby Kennedy's sites and was ordered deported to Poland. However Stacher used the Law of Return to move to Israel where he became a citizen in 1965. He died of a heart attack while on a trip to West Germany in 1977.

*****

Stardust Casino: If any one hoodlum can take claim for inventing Las Vegas, it was Tony Cornero. Tony not only built the Vegas that we know today, fittingly, he died there, dropped dead gambling at the Desert Inn, while Moe Dalitz, the Godfather of Sin City, stood in the middle of the casino floor, his fat, stubby little arm around the waist of his slim and much younger wife. Cornero had gone to the Desert Inn for a last chance meeting with Godfather of the Strip, Moe Dalitz, to beg the mobs favorite front man for financing to help him complete construction on his own Casino, the cursed Stardust. The place was scheduled to open in just two weeks, on July 13, 1955, and Cornero didn't have the cash to pay the staff or supply the house tables. He was in over his head and Dalitz and everybody else knew it. Tony was in the hole to the mob to the tune of $6,000,000 that he had already borrowed finance the Stardust, and he couldn't account for half of the cash. It was a mistake to give him the money in the first place, because Tony the Hat was no businessman, just dice jockey with high ambitions.

Cornero and Dalitz met for several long hours in a conference that went nowhere. Cornero wanted the mobs money and the mob wanted Cornero's casino, but had no intention of paying another penny for it. During a break in the meeting, Cornero went out to the floor and gambled at the crap tables and quickly fell into the hole for $10,000. Then a waitress came and handed him a tab for twenty-five dollars for the food and drinks he's had. Cornero went ballistic. He was a guest of Moe Dalitz. The waitress didn't care and Dalitz stood by and watched Tony Cornero suffer through the ultimate Vegas insult to a big timer. Cornero screamed, ranted and raved and then he grabbed his chest and fell forward on the table, desperately clutching his heart through his shirt, the dice still wrapped in a his fat, hot hands.

For decades the story circulated in the underworld that Cornero didn't die of a heart attack, that his drink had been poisoned. If he was poisoned, the answer went with him. An autopsy was never done. His body was shipped off to Los Angeles for a quick funeral where an organist from the Desert Inn knocked out a rendition of his favorite song, "The Wabash Cannon Ball" and within eight hours after he hit the cold floor of the Desert Inn. Nobody checked the contents of the 7&7 he had been sipping before he dropped dead. No one cared enough to ask any serious questions anyway. The important thing was that Tony Cornero was dead, Jake the Barber Factor, a Chicago favorite, was moved into position as the Stardust's new owner of record, and everybody in mobdom was happy. They outfit had probably set Tony up from the very beginning anyway. He never would have gotten a license to run the place because he had a long criminal record and the even longer lists of powerful political enemies he had made across the state. And he had his enemies in the underworld as well. His endless arguments with the New York syndicates over the size of the Stardust, five hundred rooms, were legendary. Myer Lansky and Frank Costello were positive that Las Vegas would never be able to attract enough gamblers to fill all of those rooms, and the Stardust would cause a glut on the market reducing prices for all the other casinos.

Cornero knew about the license problem of course, but it didn't concern him, maybe he could get a license anyway. A few million went a long way in Nevada in 1950s but the word was that Moe Dalitz had taken care of that already. There was no way that Tony Cornero was going to get a gaming license in Nevada or anywhere else. So, as the opening day drew closer, Cornero entered into talks with Dalitz about leasing the place to the Dalitz operation, and Dalitz was interested but the terms that Cornero wanted were steep, a half a million a month. So Dalitz bid his time because he knew Cornero was broke and would have to crawling back to him, and when he did, they'd handle him.

While it lasted, Cornero has an amazing life. Born Anthony Cornero Stralla in an Italian village near the Swiss border in 1895, the Cornero family had owned a large farm there but his father lost it in a card game. More bad luck came when young Tony Cornero accidentally set fire to the family harvest, driving them broke and forcing them to immigrate to San Francisco in the early 1900s. At age 16, Tony pleaded guilty to robbery and did ten months in reform school, he moved to southern California and racked up another ten arrest in ten years which included three for bootlegging and three for attempted murder. He was ambitious, but as late as 1922, Cornero was still driving a cab before he decided to branch off into the rum running business. He started with a string of small boats and smuggled high priced whisky over the Canadian border and sold it to the wealthy and better clubs in Los Angles. At the same time, Cornero ran rum from Mexico to Los Angles, his freighters easily avoiding the understaffed coast guard. Next, Tony purchased the merchant ship, the SS Lily, which he stocked with 4,000 cases of the best booze money could buy and ran the booze into Los Angles under moonlight.

In 1931, Cornero decided to switch over to gambling and moved, with his brothers, to Las Vegas and opened one of the town's first larger casinos, the Green Meadows, which was known for its staff of attractive and friendly waitresses. The Meadows turned a small, but healthy profit, and soon Cornero was investing his returns into other casinos in the state, mostly in Las Vegas. The money started to pour in, and before long, New York's Luciano, Lansky, Frank Costello sent around their representatives and demanded a cut in Cornero's action, but Cornero, who had always operated on the fringe of the national syndicate, refused to pay. Instead he had built up his own organization and was strong enough to turn the syndicate bosses down. The Syndicate, which had a small but powerful presence on the West coast, prepared for war and started by burning Cornero's Green Meadows casino to the ground. Realizing he could never win the fight, Cornero sold out his interest in Nevada and returned to Los Angles.

In 1938 Cornero bought several large ships and refurbished them into luxury casino's at a cost of over $300,000, and anchored them three miles off the coast of Santa Monica and had gamblers shuttled from shore by way of motor boats. Cornero's lead ship, The Rex, had a crew of 350, waiters' waitresses, cooks, a full orchestra, and enforcers. The first class dining room served French cuisine only and on most nights, some 2,000 patrons flooded on to the ship to gamble, dance and drink the night away. Tony was hauling in an estimated $300,000 a night after expenses, and the money would have continued to pour in, had he not become the center of a reform movement in Los Angeles County.

State Attorney General Earl Warren ordered a raid on the Rex and several other of Cornero's off coast ships. Cornero and the California government fought a series of battles, with Tony's lawyers arguing that his ships were operating in international waters, and the California government taking the indefensible stance that it didn't care where they were they were, they were still illegal. Back and forth it went, until at one point, after raiders had smashed almost a half a million worth of gambling equipment on one of his ships, Cornero decided to fight back. When the law men came to raid his ships, Cornero ordered his men to repel the attackers with water hoses. A sea battle went on for nine hours and the lawmen finally gave up. But Cornero was beaten and he knew it and he closed up his off shore operations. Tony tried to open a few gambling joints inside Los Angles, but Micky Cohen, the ruling bookie and dope dealer in the town, shut him down. When Cornero refused to back down, Cohen had his boys bomb Cornero's Beverly Hills estate. Fearing for his life, Cornero took his fortune and moved to Las Vegas.

After several years in Vegas, Cornero undertook his dream, to build the largest gambling casino-hotel in the world, the Stardust. Then he went broke. Tony went out like the gambler he was. Of the estimated $25 million he had earned his career as a gambler, Tony Cornero had less than $800 in his pockets when he died. "I got the Stardust for Chicago," Johnny Roselli bragged and for once, he may have been near the truth.

After the Las Vegas Stardust casinos original owner Tony Cornero, either died of a heart attack or was poisoned, Tony Accardo called Johnny Roselli back to Chicago for a meeting at Moe's Restaurant with Murray Humphreys and Jake Guzak. Always the hustler, Roselli knew that the bosses back in Chicago were worried because they were losing what little presence they had in Vegas, and as the power west of New York, they felt, as a matter of mob pride, that they should have a major presence on the Strip. Roselli filled them in on the situation at the Stardust. It was, as Roselli called it, a "grind joint," a paradise for the low rollers located right in the heart of the Strip. It was agreed immediately that Chicago would take the Stardust for themselves. Eventually Kansas and Milwaukee had a piece of the Stardust, but all activity in the Stardust was overseen by the Chicago family, they got paid for babysitting the action in Las Vegas but they also took a bigger cut because of it.

Fronting the entire operation would be the mob's favorite and most successful con man, John Factor, brother to cosmetic king Max Factor. John Factor, AKA "Jake the Barber" went way back with the Chicago outfit, back to the days when Johnny Torrio was running things. Humphreys either put up Chicago's money for the purchase and used Factor as its front man, or had Factor put up the purchasing money he got from Humphreys. One way or the other two things were certain. From that point on, Jake the Barber was Chicago's front man in Vegas and Chicago had the Stardust, lock, stock and barrel. And it was a mob gold mine. The Stardust boasted 1,032 rooms, and, when it opened for business in 1955, with Lyndon Baines Johnson and Bobby Baker as the guests of honor, the Stardust had one of the biggest casinos in the world. There were some luxury suites but mainly the Stardust was for low rollers. To stress that, in the back parking lot there were the cheap one-room cabins and spaces for RV units.

EXTRA

LAS VEGAS AGE

GAMBLING BILL PASSES SENATE
ASSEMBLY TO O. K. AMENDMENT

SIX COMPANIES ANNOUNCES NEW RAILWAY CONSTRUCTION | *Measure Will Become Law As Soon As Senate Amendment Passes Assembly and Signed By Governor* | SHIPS SEARCH FOR MISSING ON ICE FLOE | MAYOR WALKER SAYS HEALTH COMES FIRST

It was Dalitz's idea to set up the Stardust as a place for "low rollers" and the Desert Inn for "high rollers."   But first they would have to spruce up the Stardust in the fabled Las Vegas tradition of tacky splendor for the masses, and Murray Humphreys arranged for a million dollar loan from the Teamsters Welfare Fund by way of Red Dorfman via Jimmy Hoffa. At first, the outfit was excited at the prospect of having Jake the Barber as their front man. Jake was, if nothing else, trustworthy.

Nevada State Journal
RENO, NEVADA, FRIDAY, MARCH 20, 1931

GAMING, DIVORCE BILLS SIGNED

And the reason he was trustworthy was that he was smart enough to know the outfit would kill him in a heartbeat if he tried anything slick with them. The way the boys saw things running was that they would steal the place blind and if anything went wrong, Factor could take the fall for them. "But," wrote Hank Messeck, "he couldn't get a license either, much to the disgust of the Chicago boys. The Barber tried everything he could to get a license but there was no way it was going to happen. He finally bowed to reality and announced he would lease the Desert Inn Group." Factor said he wanted six and a half million a year for the rent but Dalitz was not about to pay that since he held all the aces in the deal including heavy clout with the Nevada state government. "It took," wrote Hank Messeck, "a western Apalachin to solve the matter." Meeting in Sidney Korshak's Beverly Hills office were Meyer Lansky, Longy Zwillman, and Doc Stacher who represented their syndicate and Moe Dalitz and Morris Klienman who represented the Desert Inn. Representing Chicago was Johnny Roselli's replacement by order of Momo Giancana, Marshal Caifano and John Bats Battaglia. It was decided that the lease on the Stardust would be $100,000 a month, a low figure for the second largest moneymaker in Las Vegas. In the end, the true owners of the Stardust were Moe Dalitz and his partners, Paul Ricca, Tony Accardo, Sam Giancana and Murray Humphreys. Other smaller point holders included Wilbur Clark and Yale Cohen.

Morris Klienman (Above)

Large or small point holders, everybody was making money off the Stardust. Carl Thomas, the master of the Las Vegas Skim, estimated that the Chicago mob was skimming $400,000.00 a month from the Stardust in the early sixties, and that was only for the one arm bandits in the casino, the blackjack game, keno and roulette and poker yielded a different and higher skim. "Everybody," Thomas said, "played with cash. You couldn't get the paddle into the slot at the craps table, there were so many hundred dollar bills crammed into the drop boxes. That's why the front men who were the big shots in town, got laws passed that kept the wise guys who were the real owners, out of town."

Freemont Street mid-1930s

As a rule, cash from the skims were paid out to each member of the Chicago operation in accordance with the number or percentage of points each person held in the casinos. Normally, only a few thousand dollars per point or percentage were paid out on a regular basis, with the bigger lump sum payments coming in March after the accountants were finished with their end-of-year figures. Then, hidden investors flew into Vegas with their girlfriends and wives to pick up their cash payments in person staying as "comped" guests all over town. Free women, free hotel suites, free gambling, and free money, free everything. For wise guys there was no place in the world like Vegas.

Ida Devine, the wife of Irving "Niggy" Devine who owned the New York Meat Company, which supplied the Las Vegas casinos, was the prime courier for the skim money out of Vegas to Chicago. She replaced Virginia Hill as Chicago deep cover operative in Vegas and chief exporter for the skimmed cash out of Vegas. Ida would take the train out of Vegas to Chicago's union station where she was normally met by one of Humphreys' people, Gus Alex or George Bieber, law partner to Mike Brodkin. From there, she was escorted to the Ambassador East Hotel on Goethe Street, not far from where Humphreys and Gus Alex lived. They would check into a room there for several hours, Chicago would receive its share of the skim money and then Ida was brought back to Union Station and placed safely on a train out of town.

By 1958, Accardo and Sam Giancana were taking $300,000.00 a month each out of Las Vegas. After a while, Giancana didn't trust anybody to bring in his share of the skim, so he went to Vegas and got it himself. Least of all, Giancana didn't trust Jake Factor and eventually assigned the Chicago outfit's "Outside man" in Vegas to follow Factor around Vegas and Beverly Hills and report his every move back to Chicago.

Murray Humphreys also stayed very close to Factor during his entire involvement in the Stardust and influenced Factor to follow through with his lease of the Stardust to Moe Dalitz's United Hotels Corporation. Sidney Korshak acted as the "go-between" for Factor and the Desert Inn Group, which was made up of Moe Dalitz and Allard Roen. The entire deal was so convoluted that the Nevada State Gaming Commission called a special meeting to look into the purchase and called Allen Roen, the Stardust representative, to answer a few questions.

Sydney Korshak, the Mob Lawyer

Moe Dalitz closed the Stardust deal in Chicago on November 5 and 6, 1960. He met with Accardo, Humphreys and Giancana and worked a deal, which would give Chicago a greater interest in the Stardust as well as the Desert Inn, the Riviera, and the Freemont. The remarkable sale of the Stardust Casino by Factor and his group to Moe Dalitz and his United Hotels happened in August of 1962 for $14,000,000.00, a relatively small amount for such a large enterprise. Eugene "Jimmy" James acted as his go between to the Teamsters fund. James was the former secretary-treasurer of the Laundry Cleaning and Dye House Workers International Union as well as the President of Local 46 of the same union. However, he was caught stealing union funds on November 17, 1960 and he was going to jail as a result. So when Humphreys approached him to act as a go for one point in the Stardust, paid to his family directly while he was in jail, James readily agreed. Tony Accardo, Paul Ricca and Murray Humphreys took at least five points each, a point being valued at $125,000.00. Another mobster named Nick Civella, got $6,000.00 a month out of the deal, paid by the casino, as a broker's fee.

When news of the transaction hit the media, that John Factor had sold out what was then one of the largest and most profitable casinos in the world for the paltry sum of $15,000,000.00, Robert Kennedy, then the Attorney General of the States, thought it was a ridiculously small sales figure and ordered an investigation to find out who really owned the Stardust and why the sale price was so small. At the same time Kennedy's Justice Department and the Nevada state gaming commission began scrutinizing the stockholding in the Stardust, they opened this investigation in search of hidden assets by Momo and other hoods. Had those investigations not been halted on the President's orders, it would have revealed that Factor was a pawn in a much larger game as well as uncovering the Teamsters enormous funds buried in the casinos by mob accountants. In September of 1962, the Federal Government decided that it wanted to talk to John Factor about his incredibly profitable deals at the Stardust Casino. They had lots of questions for Jake the Barber. Two months later, in November of 1962, Factor gave deposition in Chicago about his dealing in Las Vegas and explained that although he was the owner of record of the Stardust, and was still making money off the place, $110,000.00 a month in fact, he had leased the casino portion of the club to the Dalitz group and said that he was shocked when he found out that Moe Dalitz may have been involved with gangsters. Asked about the reported $500,000.00 finder's fee paid out by Moe Dalitz to Chicago's mob lawyer Sidney Korshak, Factor said he knew nothing about Korshak, a finder's fee or the workings of the Parvin-Dohrmann Company, the company Dalitz set up to purchase the casino from Factor. But before the Justice department/Nevada investigation could call Factor in to answer any questions the Immigration and Naturalization Service decided that Jake the Barber was an undesirable alien and made moves to deport him back to England where Jake was still wanted for his part in the stock swindles there.

At seventy years of age, John Factor, who had lived in America since at least 1919, was being booted out of the country.   It was in this atmosphere that the Los Angeles office of the INS decided to deport the seventy-year old Factor to his native England based on the 1943 conviction because it involved "moral turpitude."   George K. Rosenberg, the District Director of the INS was aware that Factor was seeking a pardon. "But because no action had been taken on Factor's pardon application, we figured that he was deportable and we moved to deport him."

On December 3, 1962, the Department of Justice requested that the Immigration and Naturalization begin proceedings to deport John Factor from the United States to England where he was a wanted felon.   Unable to show due cause why he should not be deported, Factor was ordered to surrender to the Los Angeles office of the INS on December 21, 1962, at which point he would be arrested and deported out of the country. Adding to Factor's woes was the ongoing IRS investigation into his back taxes for the years 1935 through 1939. The government wanted Factor to explain where he received $479,093.27 in income, and Factor couldn't remember. If he were deported, the Government would impound his holdings until the matter was settled.   But Factor was saved by a Presidential Pardon. Abusing the pardon privilege has a torrid and often astounding history, even on a state level. In the early 1920s, Illinois incredibly corrupt Governor, Len Small, sold an estimated 500 pardons before he was indicted and chased from office. Small's broker on the pardon deals was a union extortionist named "Umbrella Mike" Boyle, a bigwig in the Electrical Workers Union. Among Boyle's clients was Spike O'Donnell, who immediately started the great Chicago beer wars of 1926 upon his release, James "Fur" Sammons, a lunatic killer who scared even the Capone organization he worked for, and Johnny Touhy, the short-lived boss of the Terrible Touhy gang.

In the 1970's, when federal prosecutors tried to deport southwestern Pennsylvania mob boss, John S. LaRocca, Governor John Fine pardoned the alleged Godfather of corruption along with his caporegime, Frank Rosa. Later, Governor George Earle pardoned mafia boss Joe Luciano, Luigi Quaranta and alleged Caporegime Nicholas Piccolo. He also pardoned Frankie Palermo, an alleged made member of the Mafia, Felix Bocchiccio, a fight fixer, Leo Kamminski and Louie Barish, suspected mob gamblers. One of the earliest and most outrageous pardons on records belongs to Harry Truman who pardoned "Ice pick" Danny Motto, a labor thug in the Gambino family. Motto had been convicted of war time racketeering and as a result, Danny the Ice Pick wasn't allowed to hold an "elective" office in New York's Bakers union, local 350, a 900-member local which he terrorized from 1939 until his death in the 1980s. Motto's 1947 federal racketeering charge, plus a previous conviction for murder, gave the Justice Department due cause to deport the hood. However, at the last moment, when deportation had been ordered, Truman granted a pardon and the deportation was canceled. The man who worked behind the scenes on Motto's behalf was his lawyer, Herb Itkin, a shadowy figure with unspecified connections to Naval Intelligence and later to the CIA. It was Itkin who introduced New York's Lindsay administration to labor mobster, loan shark and Danny Motto's boss, Anthony "Tony Ducks' Corralo, a meeting that would eventually led to the James Marcus scandal of 1966. Truman also pardoned an enormous number of felons from the Boss Pendergast political machine. More than half of those pardoned were convicted of interfering with a citizen's right to vote, or, in other words, were members of Owney Madden's goon squads.

Richard Nixon, who was pardoned by Jerry Ford, pardoned Angelo "Gyp" DeCarlo, a capo in the Gambino crime family and a major loan shark in Northern New Jersey. Officially, DeCarlo got the pardon because he was supposed to be dying of cancer. When released however, he reentered the loan sharking business and was suspected in ordering at least one murder within the first six months of his release. In 1970, DeCarlo told an FBI undercover agent that he paid singer Frank Sinatra $150,000 in cash to give to Vice President Spiro Agnew, to secure the pardon.   Nixon also pardoned the mobs personnel loan officer, Teamster President Jimmy Hoffa in 1974. Three years later, two federal informants reported that Allen Dorfman and gangster Tony Provenzano had each collected about $500,000 in cash, which was delivered to Nixon's counsel, Charles Colson. According to the informants, the money had been skimmed off of the Vegas casinos and was a payoff for both Hoffa's release and for the restrictions on that release which forbade Jimmy from returning to the Union business   During his brief presidency, John F. Kennedy issued 472 pardons, more than any Chief Executive before or since. About half of which are appear to be questionable at best but the most outrageous is the Factor pardon.

In 1926, Factor, (AKA Jake the Barber) brother to Max Factor, conned thousands of British citizens out of $8 million dollars, (1928 value) Factor fled England for Chicago and successfully avoided extradition by paying to have himself kidnapped and accused six innocent men of the crime who served a total of 130 years for the fake abduction.   In 1942, Factor was convicted on federal charges and sentenced to ten years for a botched confidence scam. Released in 1948, Factor claimed he was broke, but, seven years later, opened the Stardust Casino in Vegas. In 1962, Factor sold his share of the casino, then the largest and most profitable in the world, for a paltry 14 million dollars. The buyer was the mobs other front man, Moe Dalitz. Chicago bosses Tony Accardo, Paul Ricca and Murray Humphreys took at least five points each from the sale, a point being valued at $125,000. Another hood, Nick Civella, got $6,000 a month out of the deal, paid by the casino, as a broker's fee.

Attorney General Robert Kennedy thought it was a ridiculously small sales figure and ordered an investigation to find out who really owned the Stardust and why the sale price was so small. At the same time, Kennedy's Justice Department and the Nevada state gaming commission, began scrutinizing the stockholders in the Stardust and opened an investigation in search of hidden assets by the Mafia. t was in this atmosphere that the Los Angeles office of the INS decided to deport the seventy year old Factor to England based on the 1943 fraud conviction. On December 3 1962, the Department of Justice requested that the Immigration and Naturalization begin proceedings to deport Factor from the United States. Unable to show due cause why he should not be deported, Factor was ordered to surrender to the Los Angeles office of the INS on December 21 1962, at which point he would be arrested and tossed out of the country. Then the Kennedy's gave John Factor a full pardon. But at what cost? The executive clemency had all the earmarks of a mob style shake down because just seven days before Bobby Kennedy's Justice Department ordered Factor deported, on November 26 1962, the Attorney General did something unusual, he changed the laws that govern Presidential pardons. It was only the second time the rules, which are actually a mere fourteen set of suggestions since they are advisory in nature, would be tampered with from 1946 until 1997. Bobby Kennedy changed the rules by cutting out the middle man, all pardon requests went directly to the White House and then to the Justice Department, not the other way around which is how it was before Factors pardon was granted. It appears that Bobby's tampering was all about money because one day a very drunken Chuckie English, one of Chicago's mob boss Sam Giancana top men, strolled out of the Armory Lounge, the outfits meeting place, and leaned against the FBI observation car parked just across the street from the tavern and started a conversation with the agents who reported "English is bemoaning the fact that the federal government is closing in on the organization and nothing can be done about it. He made several bad remarks about the Kennedy administration and pointed out that the Attorney General raising money for the Cuba invaders make's Chicago's syndicate look like amateurs"

What English was talking about in front of a bar on a cold Chicago afternoon was the same thing business executive across the country were whispering about in their paneled board rooms. Many of the nation's leading CEO's had taken phone calls and were amazed to find themselves on the other end of phone line with the Attorney General of the United States of America. They were even more amazed at what they heard. Kennedy wanted money to help rescue the Bay of Pigs survivors. The Attorney General reminded the executives that they had either pending contracts before the government or criminal cases pending, brought by the Justice department. Before they could respond, Kennedy interrupted, mentioned the fund to free the Cubans again, and hung up. Jake Factor was a rich man and nobody's fool. He threw $25,000 cash into the project and explained to a curious press that James Roosevelt, the problem child of the clan, had approached him about the donation, which he swore had nothing to do with his pardon. He was also one of Kennedy's single largest political contributors.

On December 24 1962, from his father's estate in Palm Beach Florida, John F. Kennedy signed a Presidential Pardon for Jake the Barber. Pardons are normally granted on a master warrant and although several sentence reductions were given that day on a master pardon, Factors was the only single pardon granted. The deportation proceeding against Jake was dismissed on December 26 1962, and the investigation into the Stardust casino was quietly drawn to a close. A Presidential pardon was golden but just to be sure, on July 16, 1963, in Los Angeles John Factor, the poor kid from the ghettos of Chicago, raised a slightly shaking hand and along with other more recent arrivals, took the oath of citizenship of the United States of America. "I'm the luckiest man alive," he said and he was probably right. Factor always denied that the mob used pressure with the White House to win him his pardon but in mid-1963, while Factor was trying to gain control of the National Life Insurance company of America and was buying up the company's shares at $125.00 each, he then sold 400 shares of his $125.00 a share stock to Murray Humphreys at $20.00 each. A loss of $105.00 per share to Factor. Humphreys then sold the shares back to Factor for $125.00 a share making Humphreys $42,000.00 richer in one day. As far as the Hump's unusual and creative stock transaction with Jake the Barber was concerned, the government decided that it was a taxable exchange "for services rendered" and sent tax gain bills to both them.

*****

Strawman Case One: In 1978, the Kansas City office of the FBI bugged a conversation between Mafia elders Carl "Cork" Civella and Carl "Tuffy" DeLuna. The subject of Las Vegas came up and the agents learned that Midwestern fractions of the Mafia were attempting to buy into the Argent Corporation, the holding corporations for several mob run casinos. In November of that year, 1978, agents bugged the home of a Civella relative and recorded a six-hour meeting between Nick Civella, DeLuna, Joseph Vincent Agosto, and Carl Wesley Thomas. The subject at hand was how the local Vegas hoods, Agosto and Thomas, were skimming (Stealing cash) from the count room at the Tropicana Casino. The agents learned that Agosto, who was on the casinos payroll, was the skims coordinator and Thomas oversaw the actual theft of the cash by the casinos managers in the playing area. Agosto took the money and handed it, about $80,000 per theft, to Carl Caruso, who in turn flew the money to Kansas City where the bosses took their share (About half of each delivery) and then shipped the rest off to the bosses in Chicago. On February 14, 1979, FBI agents converged on the Kansas City International Airport and arrested a mob courier carrying $80,000 in skim money. In the meantime, agents searched DeLuna's home and found the records he had kept on his expenses during the skim. The records "turned out to be devastating evidence, implicating mobsters in several cities, connecting them to the skim. The first Strawman case resulted in the indictments of the entire hierarchy of the Kansas City Family. The RICO indictments included the family's hidden interests in skimming from the Argent Corporation, the Tropicana casino, and the local bingo industry. Joe Agosto became a government witness and on September 4, 1984, Carl Civella was fined and sentenced to 10-to-30 years in prison and his son, Anthony Civella, received five years and was fined. Both DeLuna and Moretina received long sentences also.

*****

Strawman Two case: The second Strawman case, or the skimming of Las Vegas casinos by the mob, involved mostly members of the Chicago syndicate. The case was drawn together in 1978 when mobster Nick Civella called, Anthony Chiavola, a Chicago police cop, and told him that he wanted to set up a meeting at his house. The FBI intercepted the phone call and bugged the Chiavola home where the meeting was held. The four meeting revealed that Civella was trying to buy out the Chicago Family's interests in the Stardust and the Fremont casinos for $10 million dollars. Chicago's representatives rejected the bid feeling that the skim they would collect over the years would far exceed the offer. And it was all recorded on tape. During the Strawman two case, Cleveland Mafia boss, Angelo Lonardo testified for the government, making an already strong case, very strong. On Jan. 21, 1986 Joey Aiuppa, Jackie Cerone, Joseph Lombardo, and Angelo La Pietra, all of Chicago, were convicted along with Frank Balestrieri of Milwaukee.

*****

Vaci, Emil: Born 1910. Died June 6, 1986. At age 73 Vaci was a mob insider who worked as a maître d' at Ernesto's Backstreet restaurant at 3603 E. Indian School Road in Phoenix, Arizona. He'd only held the position for six months and had a side line running a Las Vegas junket business with Chicago mob burglars Paul Schiro, Richard Cleary and Carl Urbinati, all of whom had worked for Tony Spilotro. Schiro, an Arizona resident for decades, was a killer and one of Spilotro's main enforcers.

On the night of June 6, 1986, Vaci got his first and only phone call while at work. Coworkers reported that he ran to the phone and then seemed unusually happy the rest of the night. He left at 11:40 p.m., and was last seen walking toward his wife's car in the parking lot. Vaci had already testified twice before a federal grand jury investigating casino skimming and other activities by Spilotro. This time he had been granted immunity and was due to testify several days before he was killed. For a while there was speculation in law enforcement and press circles that Tony Spilotro had ordered the Vaci murder without approval from Chicago which resulted in Spilotro being killed.

Years later at the Family Secrets Trial in Chicago in 2007, mob killer Nick Calabrese described for jurors recently how he and several other alleged mob killers went about stalking Vaci for weeks in Phoenix before kidnapping him as he left his job that night. Calabrese testified that he learned alleged mob underboss Jimmy Marcello had financed the hit. Calabrese stated that the crew had ventured out west from Chicago originally to hunt down and murder Tony Spilotro because, he said "Spilotro's deals were bringing a lot of heat" on the Outfit and he also was having a fling with the wife of a casino executive, Lefty Rosenthal. However, Spilotro lived that day because they couldn't find him, instead the crew detoured to Phoenix where they planned to murder Emil Vaci. Calabrese added that Vaci "Made the people back in Chicago nervous" because he knew so much about the skim going on in Las Vegas.

Tony Spilotro

Calabrese said he was in a van parked right next to Vaci's car. Calabrese had left the van's sliding door open a crack as he waited for Vaci to leave work. He had already spread a tarp on the floor to drain in any blood. When he heard footsteps as Vaci approached the van he flung open the door and tried to get Vaci into the van. They struggled, and Joe Hansen, the van's driver and another reputed killer, came over to help. Once they got Vaci inside the van, Nick Calabrese pulled out a .22-caliber gun with a silencer, and Hansen drove off. He said that Vaci begged for his life and assumed he was being robbed and begged Calabrese to take his wallet and all his money.

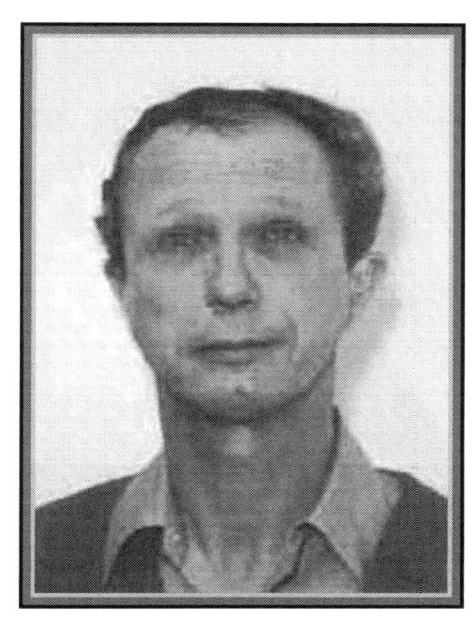

George Jay Vandermark oversaw the mob skim from the slots at the Stardust casino. He disappeared in August or September of 1976. Rumor had it that he went into hiding in Mazatlan in Mexico, or was given an all-expense paid vacation there. One way or the other, he disappeared forever. In the 1960s, Vandermark set up and managed the slots skim at the Freemont Hotel. His slots skim brought out an estimated $250,000 a week from the casinos and into the hands of the mob. When Lefty Rosenthal took over, he sent Vandermark to the Stardust to watch over the skim there. He disappeared a short time later.

"He said, 'Take my money, take my wallet,'" Calabrese recalled. "Then he said, 'Oh, no, I'm not going to say anything.'"

"Did you say anything to him?" the prosecutor asked.

"No," Calabrese said.

When Vaci realized he was going to be murdered for being subpoenaed, he broke down in tears and promised he wouldn't tell the grand jury anything. A second later, Calabrese aimed a .22 at Vaci's head and fired by the gun jammed. He fired another round through Vaci's head as he pleaded for his life. Hansen asked if Calabrese was sure Vaci was dead and Calabrese replied that he was sure he was but to be sure he shot Vaci in the head again. Although the killers had agreed to bury Vaci's body 45 minutes away in the desert and already dug the hole, they decided it was too dangerous to drive around so long with the body and simply dumped Vaci's body in a canal.

Vaci's body was found wrapped in black plastic in a dry canal bed on 48th Street on June 7, 1986. Near the body was a .38-caliber pistol that had been stolen in Chicago. The gun was empty and had not been fired recently. Investigators speculated it was left at the scene as a message that the Chicago mob was behind the killing although word on the street of Chicago was that one of the killers, probably Calabrese had accidentally dropped the gun from a jacket pocket and left it on the scene by mistake. In 2007, Paul Schiro was sentenced to five years and five months in federal prison for taking part in a nationwide jewelry-theft ring run by a former Chicago police chief of detectives. Later that he was also convicted in the Family Secrets Trial.

*****

Tocco, Joe: AKA Buddy AKA Papa Joe: Brother of Chicago mobster Albert Tocco, Joe Tocco allegedly represented the Outfits interests (Mostly real estate and political corruption) in Phoenix, Vegas and LA.

Untouchables: In the late 1950's, after the Kefauver committee's investigation into organized crime ended, the television airwaves were flooded with gangster epics, but none was as successful as "The Untouchables." A weekly feature that fictionalized the sensational doings of federal prohibition agent Elliot Ness. While there certainly no doubt that Ness and his men were heroic in their battle against the Capone mob, the fact is that Al Capone probably never knew Elliot Ness's name, since Ness and his group of so-called "Untouchables," government agents were little more than a mere nuisance to Capone organization than anything else.

Elliot Ness died in 1957, his exploits against Capone almost unknown and forgotten. However, a few days before his death, Ness's biography "The Untouchables" was published. The book, complete with occasional embellishments, sold well and Hollywood, specifically Desi-Lu productions, which was owned by Desi Arnez and Luci Ball, decided that Ness's exploits, properly rewritten, would make a fine television show. They were right. In its first season, The Untouchables, starring the stoic Robert Stack, was a smash hit.

While the program was popular with the general public, it palled with the Mafia, which still operated, more or less, as an unknown entity. What's more, the mob in 1960 was still ruled over by men who had known Capone and Nitti, who were often the focus of the show, and were fond of them. The national Mafia commission figured, correctly, that by allowing the show to air, that it would set a precedent. They reasoned, if the outfit were allowed to be discussed openly on television, what was next?

"So the council had a meet about it," wrote Lucky Luciano, "and one of the guys in Profaci's outfit named Joe Colombo come up with the idea of forming a legitimate association of Americans with Italian backgrounds to start a campaign against usin' just Italian names for them gangsters in the TV shows and movies. The whole idea was to try and get The Untouchables off the fuckin' air." The syndicate backed Colombo's idea and put money into something called the Federation of Italian American Democratic Organizations, headed by US Congressman Alfred Santangelo, who, according to Luciano, knew from the start that the entire organization was underwritten by the mob. The federation launched a boycott against the program's sponsor, Ligget & Myers Tobacco Company, who eventually withdrew their support from the show. But the boycott that was supposed to take the show off the air had just the opposite effect. When word of the Mafia-backed ban made the press, the show's rating went through the roof and Chesterfield cigarettes were back as the program's sponsor.

Elliot Ness

    Exasperated, the Chicago mob's elders put Johnny Roselli, their west coast representative, on the case. Roselli recruited L.A mobster Jimmy "The Weasel" Fratianno to fix the problem by shooting Desi Arnez, the show's primary producer. "Millions of people all over the world see this show every fucking week," Roselli told Fratianno. "It's even popular in Italy. And what they see is a bunch of Italian lunatics running around with machine guns, talking out of the corner of their mouths, slopping spaghetti like a bunch of fucking pigs. They make Capone and Nitti look like bloodthirsty maniacs. The top guys have voted a hit. We're going to clip Desi Arnez the producer of the show." Eventually, cooler heads prevailed and it was decided that killing Arnez, who was one of the world's most popular entertainment personalities, would only cause more problems than it would solve, but, still, the bosses wanted the show taken off the air. Since Arnez was leasing space to Frank Sinatra's production company at Desilu studios, where Arnez was also filming The Untouchables, Chicago's boss Tony Accardo told his underboss Sam Giancana to contact Frank Sinatra and have him talk with Arnez about taking the program off the air. Sinatra may have taken the request further then Accardo intended it to go.   In late April of 1961, Sinatra, actress Dorothy Provine and composer Jimmy Van Heusen drove to the Indian Wells Country Club outside of Las Angeles and waited in the restaurant, where Arnez ended most evenings at the bar. Almost on schedule, Arnez strolled into the club, dwarfed by his bodyguards. Spotting Sinatra, Arnez good naturedly yelled across the room, "Hi Ya Dago!" and then walked over to Sinatra's table. Sinatra was all business and got right to the point. He told Arnez that his friends didn't like the Untouchable program and that it made all Italians look like killers. Arnez, slurred with whiskey, replied: "What do you want me to do Frank, make them all Jews?" Except in his thick Cuban accent it came out "U's."

 "You want them all to be U's, Frankie? Huh? Let me tell you something, I remember you when Jew couldn't get a yob Frankie, couldn't get a yob! So why don't you forget all this bullshit and just have your drinks and enjoy yourself? Stop getting your nose in where it doesn't belong you and your so-called friends," and then walked away leaving a castrated Sinatra to say, "I couldn't hit him, we've been friends for too long."

At around 4:00 A.M. Sinatra's group left the bar and went to Van Heusen's house in Palm Desert, with Sinatra still fuming over the humiliation he had taken from Arnez. Once inside Van Heusen's house, Sinatra exploded and attacked an original painting by Norman Rockwell, carving it up with a kitchen knife. "If you try to fix that or put it back," he told Van Heusen, "I will come and blow the fucking house up."   The Untouchables not only stayed on the air, it became a classic and spawned a film and started television's love affair with gangsters.

IN THEIR OWN WORDS

"We don't get as rich as you think we do," "This is hard work. I would not do it over again. I would not want my children to do it. … The first thing I would do would be to get a good education like I am trying to give my children, and when I got real learned, I would become a United States senator like you." **Moe Sedway to the Kefauver Committee**

"And then, like Willie Alderman, you know. They had that "Ice Pick Willie" named on him, you know, don't you see, but I don't believe all that stuff. He was the nicest, kind-est-hearted man--I don't know anything about his past. From the time I knew him when he was here, I never knew a kinder-hearted man than him. Then there's another one, Dave Berman, that they said did this, that, and the other, and he was another high-class guy. And actually, when I walked in the Riviera after he died, I just always been used to seein' him, and liked him, and tears came into my eyes. I just kinda choked up. And there's another one got killed down there at Phoenix, Gus Greenbaum, that I never heard of him ever turnin' anybody down for any charitable thing, or anything like that. Good man. I have no idea why he was killed. But he was, in my way of thinkin', he was just a heck of a good man. Oh, hell, he was the best guy! He just was--just was no foolin' about it, you know, just--anything is all right. He was there. (Bugsy Siegel) I barely knew him. But, actually, he was another one, most accommodating, most likable fellow, had the best personality you ever seen. And if he was a bad guy, he damn sure didn't show it from the outside." **Las Vegas casino owner, Benny Binion**

"There were times when I thought I would die in that desert. (Back then) Vegas was a horrible place" **Meyer Lansky on building the gaming industry in Las Vegas in the 1930s. Contrary to legend, it was Lansky, not Siegel, who envisioned what Las Vegas would become.**

"What I had in mind was to build the greatest, most luxurious hotel casino in the world and invite people from all over America — maybe the high rollers from all over the world — to come and spend their money there," **Meyer Lanksy on building Las Vegas.**

"Nobody will ever believe this, but I never had any idea that Chicago and Kansas City and Milwaukee were running the Stardust, Fremont, Marina, and Hacienda. I didn't know that. I knew that (Allen) Glick was there, and I thought that he was the boss. And I knew that (lefty) Rosenthal exercised some influence, but I never knew to what degree. I knew that Rosenthal had known (Tony) Spilotro, but I never really thought that Rosenthal was part of Chicago. I mean, I knew he had associates back then' **Mob lawyer Oscar Goodman.**

'Tell the truth, didn't you give the okay to get Ben Siegel hit?'

"Lansky had been smiling, and now his face became straight. The eyes became small ice ponds.

"'He was the best friend I ever had,' Lansky said. 'His grandchildren are coming to visit with me. Why don't you stay here a few days and see for yourself? How could I get a guy killed if I have his grandchildren coming to visit me?' Lansky's eyes kept staring.

"'That was when I knew that he had Siegel killed,' **Writer Sid Zion on a conversation with Meyer Lansky**

"Well, if he wasn't a Consigliere, he was the closest goddamn thing to it." **A member of the FBI's Organized crime strike force on mob lawyer Oscar Goodman**

"There is a tendency to dismiss as inconsequential the tremendous influence and power wielded inside and outside the underworld by Morris Shenker, a functionary for the St. Louis, Kansas City, Chicago and other families. This largely was because most local law enforcement officers were unable to comprehend the complexity of the man and his operations. Shenker, a lawyer who once represented Jimmy Hoffa, was a mover and shaker and a financial genius of the caliber of Lansky. It was Shenker who tapped the Teamster Union's Central States Pension Fund to finance much of the mob's penetration of Las Vegas casinos and other ventures. Shenker's influence extended far beyond the underworld and he was able to get two of his own federal indictments killed. St. Louis underworld interests controlled two Las Vegas casinos — the Dunes, owned by Shenker, and the Aladdin." **St. Louis Post-Dispatch reporter Ronald J. Lawrence on Morris Shenker, a legendary Las Vegas underworld figure.**

"I got a kick out of having a big bankroll in my pocket. Even if I only made a couple hundred dollars, I'd always keep it in fives and tens so it'd look big." **Mickey Cohen**

"I started rooting - you know, sticking up joints - with some older guys. By now I had gotten a taste of what the racket world really was - the glamour, the way they dressed, the way they always had a pocketful of money." **Mickey Cohen**

"I never killed a guy who didn't deserve it." **Mickey Cohen**

"Don't lie. Tell one lie, then you gotta tell another lie to compound on the first." **Meyer Lansky**

"Don't worry, don't worry. Look at the Astors and the Vanderbilt's, all those big society people. They were the worst thieves-and now look at them. It's just a matter of time." **Meyer Lansky**

"Always overpay your taxes. That way you'll get a refund." **Meyer Lansky**

"All pro sports, as well as the NCAA, should thank God every day we have sports betting here... We have the only agency in the world that regulates the honesty of games." **Meyer Lansky**

"It's the first time in my life I've ever seen a dead man convicted of his own murder. So far as that jury's concerned, Johnny just walked too close to that knife." **Mickey Cohen on the death of his driver Johnny Stompanato**

"You could've made me more sympathetic" **Meyer Lansky to actor Lee Strasberg who portrayed Lansky in the film The Godfather Part 11**

"As big as US Steel? No we're bigger than US Steel." **Meyer Lansky to his wife (and an FBI microphone) as he watched a TV The David Susskind Show that claimed that organized crime could be almost as large as the US Steel Corporation.**

"Nobody will ever believe this, but I never had any idea that Chicago and Kansas City and Milwaukee were running the Stardust, Fremont, Marina, and Hacienda. I didn't know that. I knew that (Allen) Glick was there, and I thought that he was the boss. And I knew that (lefty) Rosenthal exercised some influence, but I never knew to what degree. I knew that Rosenthal had known (Tony) Spilotro, but I never really thought that Rosenthal was part of Chicago. I mean, I knew he had associates back then' **Mob lawyer Oscar Goodman.**

"The stage was decorated with a swastika and a picture of Hitler. The speakers started ranting. There were only fifteen of us, but we went into action. We ... threw some of them out the windows. . . . Most of the Nazis panicked and ran out. We chased them and beat them up. . . . We wanted to show them that Jews would not always sit back and accept insults." **Gangster Meyer Lansky recalling how he and his goons broke up a Brown Shirt rally in the Yorkville section of Manhattan**

*****

Printed in Great Britain
by Amazon